Praise for Katie Bonner

GW00646271

"Cozy readers everywhere h~~ fallen in love with Lor~~
raine Bartlett's *A Crafty Kill* ~~ing and the inhabitants~~
Victoria Square, a charming and sometimes dangerous~~
berg featuring one-of-a-kind businesses like Artisans
Alley. In **Recipes To Die For**, Katie Bonner and the rest of
the locals from Victoria Square invite you into their
kitchens to share tantalizing recipes and intimate stories
about food, family, and life. So tie on your apron and
sharpen your knives, because **Recipes To Die For** is
chock full of culinary treasures such as Andy Rust's Cinnamon Rolls, Vance Ingram's Barbequed Ribs, and Sweet
Sue's Toffee Squares. And you don't want to miss Aunt
Lizzie's Cream Scones. They're to die for!"
—*Ellery Adams, author of the Charmed Pie Mysteries*

"It doesn't get any better than this! We already love
Lorraine Bartlett's books, but now, sharing recipes from
her Artisans Alley series, she's really outdone herself.
These are wonderful, real, delicious recipes to enjoy
while we read her fabulous stories. Well done!"
—*Julie Hyzy, bestselling author of the Manor House Mysteries and White House Mystery series*

A CRAFTY KILLING

"With a cast of personable characters, and a lively, fast-
paced storyline, readers will be enthralled and delighted
with this fresh new series."
—*Fresh Fiction*

"Bartlett has crafted an ingenious venue for her wonderful new series."
—*Mystery Scene Magazine*

Other Titles by Lorraine Bartlett

The Victoria Square Mysteries
A CRAFTY KILLING
THE WALLED FLOWER (2012)
ONE HOT MURDER (2013)
Short Stories
WE'RE SO SORRY, UNCLE ALBERT
AN UNCONDITIONAL LOVE
ARE YOU LONELY TONIGHT?
PRISONER OF LOVE

Writing as L.L. Bartlett
The Jeff Resnick Mysteries
MURDER ON THE MIND
DEAD IN RED
CHEATED BY DEATH
BOUND BY SUGGESTION
Short Stories
BAH! HUMBUG
COLD CASE
WHEN THE SPIRIT MOVES YOU
ABUSED: A DAUGHTER'S STORY

Writing As Lorna Barrett
The Booktown Mysteries
MURDER IS BINDING
BOOKMARKED FOR DEATH
BOOKPLATE SPECIAL
CHAPTER & HEARSE
SENTENCED TO DEATH
MURDER ON THE HALF SHELF

RECIPES TO DIE FOR

A
VICTORIA
SQUARE
COOKBOOK

Lorraine Bartlett

Polaris Press

ISBN: 978-1466293687

Polaris Press
P.O. Box 230
North Greece, NY 14515-0230

ACKNOWLEDGMENTS

I wish to thank my faithful first readers, Dru-Ann Love and Jennifer Stanley, for finding typos and making suggestions that helped improve the book. My copyeditor Jan Freeman was a joy to work with, and the always gracious and generous Pat Ryan designed the cover and the lovely cookbook logo. Julie Hyzy gave me one of her formatting secrets for the e version and a lovely blurb. Frank Solomon did the layout and design for the print edition, and contributed a number of pieces of art.

Thank you all.

TABLE OF CONTENTS

INTRODUCTION
By Katie Bonner
Manager, Artisans Alley, Victoria Square

Hello, my name is Katie Bonner and I love to bake. There, I said it. I'll also tell you that there was a time when I didn't like to cook, but I'm getting better at it. (For me, baking and cooking are entirely different things.)

I led a perfectly ordinary life until the day I inherited another forty-five percent of Artisans Alley on lovely Victoria Square in McKinlay Mill, New York.

Okay, back up. I led a perfectly ordinary life until my husband Chad invested our life savings (and without my input) in Artisans Alley, the big craft arcade in the old applesauce warehouse on Victoria Square in the village of McKinlay Mill, New York. It was money we had been saving to open a bed and breakfast. I was to be the force behind the scenes, while Chad would act as host. I'd do the paperwork, coordinate the marketing, the staff, and the cooking, while Chad would pour the sherry and tell amusing anecdotes to our guests.

Chad's investment (or ten percent ownership) put a deep strain on our marriage. Still, we were close to a reconciliation when Chad died in a car wreck.

Instead of baking for my guests at The English Ivy Inn, I now bake for my vendors at Artisans Alley. Baking gets me through the tough times. Losing my life savings . . . losing Chad . . . and the deaths that have happened on Victoria Square. Um . . . there seem to be a lot of them. In case you haven't read about them, they've been chronicled in several books. (*A Crafty Killing, The Walled Flower*, and *One Hot Murder*.)

Ahem ... as I was saying.... I know you're probably thinking ... cooking/baking ... what's the difference?

There *is* a difference. When I cook, I'm usually hungry and don't have the patience to wait. (Again, I'm getting better at that.) But when I bake, I like to experience every part of the procedure. From preheating the oven, to measuring and mixing the ingredients, inhaling the intoxicating aroma of freshly baked goodies, to serving the bread, cookies, cakes, or pies I make. There's a ceremony involved. I bake for pleasure, I bake for sustenance, I bake because I enjoy it.

It was my great-aunt Lizzie who taught me everything I know about baking. My aunt was an old maid—something she found terribly shameful. She'd been engaged, but her heart was broken when her sweetheart was killed in a work accident. She came to the U.S. from Scotland to start a new life at least twenty years before I was born to her brother's son. "Back home," as she used to say, she worked as a cook in a pub. After she arrived in the States, she found work in diners or restaurants, either cooking or serving.

I barely remember my parents, who were killed in a car accident when I was a child. Since they had already lost their parents, there was only one person left to take me in—my father's aunt.

Aunt Lizzie, a gray-haired and imposing woman, was already in her sixties when I arrived on her doorstep. She seemed pretty grim, and I was an unhappy, solemn-eyed five-year old. Our first few days together were filled with tears (from both of us) and shouting matches. When angry, her Scottish accent was so thick I couldn't understand a word she said. The poor woman was at her wits end after one particularly long day of childcare—at a time in life when she should have been relaxing—so she pulled out the flour and sugar to bake some scones for the next morning's breakfast.

I defied her by sneaking out of my bed and watching with wide eyes as she measured the flour, the sugar, cracked an egg, and mixed them and some other ingredients with a long wooden spoon in an old yellow bowl. She had to have known I was there, peeking around the doorjamb, but she didn't say a word during the whole operation.

After the scones went into the oven, she cleaned up the kitchen and washed the bowls and utensils. She didn't seem quite so threatening as she hummed while she worked, and finished those tasks just as the piping hot scones came out of the oven.

Still steaming, they rested on a wire rack to cool. I'd never seen such a concoction before. Both of my parents worked, and all my birthday cakes had come from a bakery or grocery store. Home baking was something foreign and new to me.

Aunt Lizzie puttered around in that kitchen for what seemed liked forever, making herself a pot of tea, and setting the table. Finally she plopped two scones on a plate and set it on the table.

"You can come out now," she said, and I timidly entered the kitchen.

She sat at the table and split one of the scones, applying a thick layer of sweet butter on it, then raspberry jam, and then some goopy looking stuff which turned out to be her version of clotted cream. She placed it on a plate and poured us both a cup of tea. (Mine was ninety percent milk.)

I remember taking a reluctant bite of that still warm scone, wondering if it would taste like liver . . . but it didn't. It was sweet, and light, and wonderful on the tongue. From that moment on, tasting a scone would always fill me with a feeling of coming home.

At that moment, sharing that scone, my aunt Lizzie and I became life-long friends.

Because I was seeking a bachelor's and then a master's degree in marketing during most of our marriage, my late husband Chad did most of the cooking. He was grounded in American fare with no desire to eat the food I'd grown up with, so I let him do most of the cooking. Our meals consisted of meat, starch, and a vegetable, or one of the one-dish casseroles he'd grown up eating. He'd make mac and cheese from (*shudder*) a blue box, or tuna noodle casserole once if not twice a week. He thrived on beef, a potato, and corn—night after night after night. When he left our home, my dinners tended to be something fast and easy. Peanut butter and jelly or ham and cheese sandwiches. Cooking for one is definitely no fun.

Until recently, I continued with just a sandwich and soup for dinner. But something had to give. It isn't healthy to eat like that, and it gets boring.

That's why I decided to start making the kinds of food I grew up with. The food my aunt Lizzie taught me to make. I fondly remember the times we cooked or baked together and laughed, and enjoyed life together. She never had her own children, but she brought me up to be like her. Stubborn, independent, and . . . if I say so myself . . . a pretty good baker. And now I'm working on becoming more than just an adequate cook. To do that, I decided to put together a collection of my favorite recipes and those of the friends I've made on Victoria Square.

Enjoy!

Katie

SIGNATURE BEVERAGES

Have you met the Artisans Alley vendors and the shop owners on Victoria Square? Everyone who contributed a recipe to this book has some connection to Victoria Square.

I thought it would be nice to introduce my friends to you with their favorite beverage recipes—and everyone of them had a favorite drink and/or signature cocktail. (And, of course, you can meet them yourself in the novels: *A Crafty Killing, The Walled Flower,* and *One Hot Murder.*)

You'll notice that a lot of these beverages are alcoholic in nature. What can I say? Has being a part of Victoria Square driven a number of us to drink? Possibly. There have been several murders in our little village of late, which hadn't seen a killing in decades. But I prefer to think of the good times we've had on the Square and the reasons we've gathered together to celebrate: our Dickens Festival, the potluck dinners we've held, bridal showers, and other parties.

There's something here for everyone. Maybe you'll find something that will become your signature beverage.

BLACK WIDOW

Like me, Andy Rust is one of the youngest entrepreneurs on Victoria Square. He owns and runs Angelo's Pizzeria and is my . . . boyfriend . . . significant other . . . best friend. "A black widow?" I asked. "Isn't that a strange drink for a young guy like you?" Andy said, "My grandfather made me one on my 21st birthday. It was my first legal drink." (I didn't bother to ask if he'd been imbibing beforehand. I think we all know the answer to that.)

INGREDIENTS
juice from half a lime
½ teaspoon confectioners' sugar
¼ ounce Southern Comfort
1 ounce gold rum

In a cocktail shaker, combine all ingredients and ice. Shake well. Strain and pour into a sour glass.

BLOODY MARY

Dennis Wheeler owns Wood U, a gift shop on Victoria Square that features all things made of (what else?) wood. He has a signature product—his double-decker, inlaid-with-lots-of-pretty-woods jewelry boxes. (My late husband Chad gave me one for my birthday several years back.) And like his signature product, Dennis has a signature drink. Said Dennis, "My wife Abby and I like to go out for brunch, and a Bloody Mary is my drink of choice for that occasion. One is enough for me, and seems to taste best with eggs Benedict."

INGREDIENTS
¼ ounce lemon juice
Worcestershire sauce
celery salt
ground pepper
Tabasco
1 ½ ounce vodka
4 ounces tomato juice
celery stalk

In a tall glass, combine the first 7 ingredients over ice cubes. Garnish with the celery stalk.
Yield: 1 serving.

BULL SHOT

Vance Ingram probably knows more about Artisans Alley and its workings than anyone on the planet—and that includes me. I consider him my right-hand man when it comes to unjamming a cash register or coaxing a little more heat out of the furnace. Vance chose a Bull Shot for his signature drink. "When I was a kid, my Dad used to make this drink after being out in the cold shoveling the driveway. When I grew up I bought myself a snow blower, but I also followed in his footsteps with this drink. The directions say to drink it cold, but I like to warm the bouillon in the microwave. You can drink it either way and it still tastes fine."

INGREDIENTS
1 ¾ - 2 ounces vodka
3 ½ ounces beef bouillon

Prepare the bouillon with a lot of celery and taste test it while cooking—not afterward. Stir the vodka and cold beef bouillon in a small highball glass.
Yield: 1 serving.

COZY COCOA

What better way is there to start a cold winter morning than with something hot and delicious to drink? I'm a fan of anything with chocolate, so on the top of my list is this homemade cocoa, just the way my aunt

 Lizzie used to make it. More often than not, I'd walk home from the neighborhood elementary school, arrive half frozen, and knew I'd find my aunt standing at the stove stirring milk in a pot.

INGREDIENTS
3 tablespoons unsweetened cocoa powder
¼ cup sugar
4 cups milk
¼ teaspoon vanilla

Blend the cocoa and sugar in a small bowl. In a medium saucepan, heat the milk to scalding. Mix about ⅓ cup of the hot milk into the cocoa-sugar mixture, then pour the cocoa mixture into hot milk in the saucepan; stir until well blended. Stir in the vanilla. Serve with a dollop of whipped cream. Mmm. Delicious!
Yield: 4 servings.

CHAMPAGNE PUNCH

Gilda Ringwald, owner of Gilda's Gourmet Basket, loves the finer things in life. Perhaps that's why she excels at making the lovely baskets filled with fabulous goodies for her shop. Apparently Gilda is known for her champagne punch, and when I asked what beverage she would like to be known by, this is the recipe she gave me. It's great for showers and weddings, too!

INGREDIENTS
4 cups orange juice
1 cup ruby red grapefruit juice
½ cup lemon juice
½ cup lime juice
2 bottles (750 milliliters each) champagne, chilled

In a 2-quart pitcher, combine the juices. Refrigerate until chilled. Just before serving, stir in champagne. Serve in champagne glasses.
Yield: 3 quarts.

BANANA MILKSHAKE

Truthfully, Nona Fiske, owner of Victoria Square's needlecraft shop, The Quiet Quilter, and I are not the best of friends. She wasn't happy when I took over as the head of Victoria Square's Merchants Association, and disagreed with some of the decisions I made as executor of Ezra Hilton's will. But when she heard I was putting this cookbook together she actually called me and asked if she could contribute a recipe. I'm all for mending fences and gladly accepted. Here's the drink she identifies herself with. (Maybe because she's a little bananas herself.)

INGREDIENTS
2 small ripe bananas
1 ½ cups milk
2 cups vanilla ice cream

Cut each banana into coins. Place bananas and milk into a blender. Cover with the top and blend until smooth. Add the ice cream and blend until mixed but not pureed. Serve immediately.
Yield: 4 cups.

BRANDY MILK PUNCH

Edie Silver was the first of the new vendors who joined Artisans Alley only hours after I became its manager. She likes to think of herself as a "pistol," and what pistol-packing mama wouldn't like a signature drink with a bit a bit of a punch? Of course, depending on her mood, Edie has been known to raise and lower the amounts of liquor in this lively drink. But for the most part, she makes it like this.

INGREDIENTS
3 cups vanilla ice cream
1 cup milk
¼ cup light rum
3 tablespoons bourbon
2 tablespoons brandy
ground nutmeg

Combine the ice cream, milk, rum, bourbon, and brandy in the container of a blender. Process until smooth. Pour into glasses. Sprinkle each serving with nutmeg. Serve immediately.
Yield: 1 quart.

CHOCOLATE MILK

Ida Mitchell, one of the very first vendors to sign on at Artisans Alley, insisted I include her recipes in this collection. Ida is . . . special. (I'm not exactly sure what her problem is, but she definitely has one.) In an effort to be inclusive, I have added her signature drink. This is what she told me (verbatim).

INGREDIENTS
milk
chocolate milk powder

"Pour milk into a tall glass. Take a spoon out of your silverware drawer. Open the container of chocolate milk powder. Add two spoonfuls (tablespoons?) of chocolate milk powder. Stir. Put the spoon into the dishwasher. Drink the chocolate milk. It goes good with cookies and cake. Put the glass in the dish-washer. Go on with your day."
Yield: 1 serving.

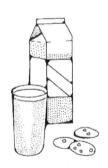

CORPSE REVIVER

When I asked Conrad Stratton, the wine merchant from The Perfect Grape on Victoria Square, what his favorite drink was, of course he answered wine. But as he doesn't grow his own grapes, nor make his own wine, he told me about a drink he learned to love when he was in France learn-ing his trade. When I first heard the name of the drink, I thought he was trying to be funny—making mock of the deaths on Victoria Square—but in fact he showed me a drink mixing guide which did indeed back up his claim.

INGREDIENTS
¾ ounce Pernod
champagne
lemon Juice

Pour the Pernod into a champagne flute, fill with champagne, sprinkle on a little lemon juice. Voila! Yield: 1 serving.

FAUX EGGNOG

Artisans Alley's resident weaver, Gwen Hardy, brought this to the Alley during our first Dickens Festival. I was surprised at how good it tasted, since it wasn't made with raw eggs as in traditional recipes, and it's so much better than the commercial product you get at the grocery store during the holidays. Try it—I'm sure you'll like it, too!

INGREDIENTS
2 quarts milk, cold
1 package (3.4 ounces) instant vanilla pudding mix
¼ cup granulated sugar
1 teaspoon ground nutmeg
1 teaspoon vanilla extract
1 cup whipping cream
additional nutmeg, optional
1 cup dark rum (optional)

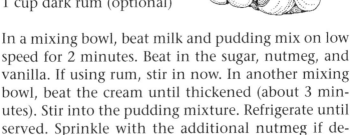

In a mixing bowl, beat milk and pudding mix on low speed for 2 minutes. Beat in the sugar, nutmeg, and vanilla. If using rum, stir in now. In another mixing bowl, beat the cream until thickened (about 3 minutes). Stir into the pudding mixture. Refrigerate until served. Sprinkle with the additional nutmeg if desired.
Yield: 2½ quarts.

FRESH BERRY TEA

Charlotte Booth owns and operates Booth's Jellies and Jams on Victoria Square. Since the basis of most of her products are the farm-fresh fruits from around the area, it's no wonder her favorite drink is made from berries. Charlotte says, "The prime ingredients for this recipe are only available in the early summer, but it's well worth the wait. Mint grows wild in my kitchen garden, so I always have plenty to use as a garnish."

INGREDIENTS
2 cups raspberries
2 cups blackberries
1 ½ cups sugar
1 cup fresh lemon juice
3 large tea bags (orange pekoe works fine)
12 cups water, divided in half
1 tablespoon fresh chopped mint

Brew the tea in 6 cups of boiled water for approximately 10 minutes. Remove from heat. In a large bowl, combine the berries, lemon juice, chopped mint and sugar and mix. Try to extract as much berry juice as possible while mixing. Remove the tea bags from brew. Add to berry mixture and let it sit for an hour. Strain the tea blend to remove pulp, seeds, and other solids. Add 6 cups of cold water. Transfer to a large pitcher. Chill and serve with a sprig of fresh mint as a garnish.
Yield: 1 gallon

HOT COGNAC CHOCOLATE

Fred Cunningham is the best real estate agent in McKinlay Mill. Okay, he's just about the *only* real estate agent in McKinlay Mill—or at least the only one who represents both residential and commercial properties. He does this winter, spring, summer, and fall. At the end of a hard day of showing houses or a retail space, Fred relaxes with a drink. In the winter, it's hot cognac chocolate. He says it's the perfect nightcap.

INGREDIENTS
4 cups milk
4 ounces semisweet chocolate chips
2 tablespoons granulated sugar
5 tablespoons cognac
6 tablespoons whipped cream, to decorate
4 teaspoons unsweetened cocoa, for sprinkling

Pour the milk into a saucepan and bring to a boil, then remove from the heat. Place the chocolate in a small saucepan and add 2 tablespoons of the hot milk. Stir over low heat until the chocolate has melted. Stir the chocolate mixture into the remaining milk and add the sugar. Stir in the cognac and pour into 4 heatproof glasses. Top each with a swirl of whipped cream and sprinkle with a little sifted unsweetened cocoa.
Yield: 4 Servings.

MANHATTAN

My attorney (and, in fact the only attorney in McKinlay Mill) sent me this note when I asked him to tell me his favorite drink: "After a long day at the office, I look forward to catching up with the morning papers and savoring a Manhattan. My dad, who was also an attorney, always drank a Manhattan in the evening and when I have one, I always think of him. So, here's to you, Dad!"

INGREDIENTS
2 ounces bourbon or blended whiskey
½ ounce sweet vermouth
a dash of Angostura bitters
maraschino cherry

In a cocktail shaker combine the bourbon or whiskey, vermouth, and bitters. Add ice cubes; cover and shake until very cold. Strain liquid into a chilled stem glass (up) or a glass filled with additional ice cubes (on the rocks). Garnish with a cherry.
Yield: 1 serving.

MINT ICED TEA

Rose Nash was the first vendor I met at Artisans Alley (and don't tell anyone, but she's my favorite vendor, too, not just because she always volunteers to work extra shifts, but she's also always ready to help pitch in for whatever needs to be done—even cleaning the bathroom). Rose is a Lady with a capital L and this is her favorite iced tea recipe, which is sweet, lovely—and a little old fashioned—just like Rose.

INGREDIENTS
3 peppermint-flavored tea bags
7 cups boiling water
1 cup cranberry juice
¾ cup lemonade concentrate

Steep the tea bags in boiling water for 5 to 10 minutes. Discard the tea bags. Pour the tea into a pitcher or large bowl. Stir in the cranberry juice and lemonade concentrate. Cover and refrigerate overnight. Serve over ice.
Yield: 8 servings.

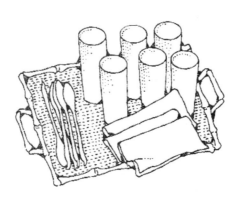

MINT JULEPS

Some of the Artisans Alley vendors have become my very good friends. One of them is Vance Ingram, who I think of as my right-hand man. Likewise, the vendors' spouses and significant others became friends, too. Vance's wife Janey made this recipe during a party they held during the Kentucky Derby. It went down very nicely on that lovely warm spring day.

INGREDIENTS
12 cups bourbon
2 tablespoons sugar
3 cups water
fresh mint leaves
finely crushed ice
fresh mint sprigs

Place the bourbon in the freezer 24 hours prior to preparing mint juleps (the bourbon won't freeze, but it will acquire a syrup-like consistency). For each serving, place ¼ teaspoon sugar in a julep cup. Add 2 tablespoons water and 7 fresh mint leaves. Stir gently until the sugar is dissolved. Add ½ cup bourbon to each cup, stirring gently. Add enough finely crushed ice to fill the cup; stir gently. Place in the freezer, and freeze for at least 3 hours. Before serving, break the ice with a spoon, then garnish each julep with fresh mint sprigs.
Yield: 24 servings.

RUSTY NAIL

Jordan Tanner and his wife Ann own Victoria Square's bakery simply called "Tanner's." Along with all their fabulous baked goods, they serve coffee, teas, and cocoa. But after a long day of baking and manning the cash register, Jordan likes to come home, put his feet up, and relax with a Rusty Nail. It's simple to make and easy to enjoy.

INGREDIENTS
1 ounce Scotch
1 ounce Drambuie

Fill a highball glass with ice. Pour the Scotch and Dambuie. Stir. Enjoy.
Yield: 1 serving.

SCOFFLAW

Detective Ray Davenport of the Monroe County Sheriff's office was assigned to investigate Ezra Hilton's death. Since then we've met on a number of occasions. In fact, he's practically become a fixture on Victoria Square. That's why I asked if he would like to contribute to this book. At first he was (surprise!) grumpy and said no, but then he called me back and said he would like to be included. When I asked for a signature beverage he came up with this recipe. He said during his tenure at the Sheriff's Office he'd come up with more than his fair share of scofflaws.

INGREDIENTS
¼ ounce of lemon juice
a dash of grenadine
1 ounce dry vermouth
1 ounce Canadian whisky
dash of orange bitters

Combine all ingredients over ice in a mixing glass. Strain the drink into a chilled cocktail glass.
Yield: 1 serving.

THE QUEEN ELIZABETH
(WHISKEY SOUR)

Liz Meier is Artisans Alley's resident stained glass artist. She makes beautiful sun catchers, ornaments, and stained glass panels of vibrant gardens and wildlife. She also repairs vintage stained glass win-

dows. When she's not in her workshop, she's the queen of her suburban palace. Her husband calls her Queen Elizabeth and makes her favorite drink when the occasion demands it.

INGREDIENTS
¾ ounce lemon juice
1 teaspoon confectioners' sugar
½ ounce bourbon (or blended whiskey)
1 stemmed cherry
1 lemon slice

In a cocktail shaker filled with ice, combine the first 3 ingredients. Strain into a short glass and add a cherry. Decorate glass with the lemon slice.
Yield: 1 serving.

ZOMBIE

I must admit that when Luther Collier from Collier's Funeral Home contacted me about contributing to this book, I was a bit taken aback. Yes, he's a very sweet man, and yes he took care of my husband when he passed. I was even more surprised when he volunteered his signature cocktail. The Zombie. Maybe he needs something that strong after working with the dearly departed all day. Or maybe he drinks them in hopes of keeping zombies *away* from his funeral parlor.

INGREDIENTS
1 ¼ ounce lemon juice
dashes of grenadine
¾ ounce blood orange juice
¾ ounce Cherry Heering
¾ ounce dark rum
¾ ounce high-proof dark rum.

Fill a cocktail shaker with ice cubes. Combine all ingredients. Shake the shaker, strain the drink into a large highball glass over crushed ice.
Yield: 1 serving.

BREAKFAST

BRAN MUFFINS WITH MOLASSES AND RAISINS

They say the way to a man's heart is through his stomach. It worked for me when I wanted to get to know my future husband, Chad. But it also works when you want to make new friends. Many's the time I brought in cookies and muffins to school—and then to college—in an effort to break the ice. And what better way to start the day than with a healthy bran muffin—it tastes good and it's good for you.

INGREDIENTS
1 cup bran flour
1 cup all-purpose white flour
4 teaspoon baking powder
½ teaspoon salt
1 cup of milk (2% or fat-free works fine)
½ cup molasses
1 egg (well beaten)
1 tablespoon melted butter*
½ cup raisins
Shortening or paper muffin liners

Grease and lightly flour your muffin tins or use paper liners. Preheat oven to 325°. In a large bowl, mix together the flour, the baking powder and the salt. Slowly add the bran flour and mix together thoroughly. Add in the molasses, the milk, the egg, and mix well. Mix in the melted butter. Fold in the raisins. Pour into muffin tins until approximately ¾ full. Bake for approximately 30 minutes or until a toothpick inserted into the middle comes out clean. Cool completely on baking rack before storing. They freeze nicely for up to a month. (*To cut calories, you can substitute the same amount of unsweetened applesauce for the butter.)

Yield: 12 muffins

ANDY'S CINNAMON BUNS

If there's one thing Andy Rust knows about, it's bread dough. He's a wiz when it comes to making dough for his pizzeria, Angelo's, right on the west edge of Victoria Square. But Andy has other culinary expertise, too. And I'm happy to share his cinnamon bun recipe with you here.

INGREDIENTS
3 ½ to 4 cups all-purpose flour
1 package active dry yeast
½ cup warm water (105 to 115 degrees)
¾ cup lukewarm milk (scalded then cooled)
⅓ cup butter, softened
⅓ to ½ cup sugar (the more, the sweeter)
½ teaspoon salt
1 egg

CINNAMON MIXTURE
2 tablespoons margarine or butter, softened
½ cup sugar
2 teaspoons ground cinnamon
¼ teaspoon cardamom powder
½ cup raisins (optional)
½ cup chopped walnuts (optional)

GLAZE
1 cup confectioners' sugar
1 tablespoon milk
½ teaspoon vanilla

Dissolve the yeast in warm water in a large bowl. Stir in the milk, sugar, butter, salt, egg, and 2 cups of the flour. Beat until smooth.

Turn the dough onto lightly floured surface.

Knead in enough remaining flour to make a soft dough that is smooth and elastic, from 3 to 5 minutes. Place in a greased bowl; turn greased side up. Cover and let rise in a warm place until the dough has doubled in size (about 1 ½ hours—the dough is ready if an indentation remains when touched).

Punch down the dough. Turn the dough onto a lightly floured surface, then roll the dough into a rectangle about 9-x-18-inches. Once rolled out spread with butter. Mix sugar, cinnamon and cardamom powder together in small dish. Sprinkle over rectangle. If you are adding raisins and/or chopped nuts, sprinkle over the cinnamon mixture before rolling up. Roll up tightly, beginning at the wide (18-inch) side.

Seal well by pinching the edges of roll together. Stretch the roll to make even. Cut the roll into 1 ½ to 2 inch slices. Place a little apart on a greased pan or cookie sheet. Cover and let the dough rise until double in bulk (about 35 to 40 minutes). Heat the oven to 375°. Bake until golden brown, 25-30 minutes.

Glaze: Mix the confectioners' sugar, milk, and vanilla until the glaze is smooth and of desired consistency. If it's too thick, add a little more milk. Spread rolls with glaze while warm.

Yield: Makes 12.

BANANA BREAD

Food and fond memories are closely associated. One of the first things I baked on my own (although my aunt Lizzie was hovering over me like a mother hen) was banana bread. My aunt never wasted anything, and when several bananas got too soft to eat, she suggested I make this easy quick bread. Every time I make it, I think of my aunt's wrinkled face and her beautiful smile of pride as she watched me work in her cozy kitchen.

I can remember helping my aunt Lizzie make banana bread many times while growing up. We'd eat it warm from the oven and spread it with butter. Delicious!

INGREDIENTS
2 ½ cups flour
1 cup sugar
3 ½ teaspoons baking powder
⅓ cup oil*
¾ cup milk
1 teaspoon vanilla
1 egg
1 cup chopped walnuts (optional)
1-2 cups mashed bananas (the more you use, the moister it will be)

Preheat oven to 350°. Spray 2 loaf pans with cooking spray, dust with flour. Measure all ingredients and place them in a large bowl. With an electric mixer, blend on medium speed and scrape the sides of the bowl often. Pour into the pans. Bake 55-60 minutes until a toothpick comes out clean. Cool on a rack. Slice to serve. (*For fewer calories, you can substitute unsweetened applesauce for the oil—it'll taste just as good!) It freezes well, too.
Yield: 12 slices.

HOMEMADE GRANOLA

Are you like me and trying to eat healthier? I don't always succeed, but a couple of years ago I decided to try and make my own granola. Not only is it a lot cheaper than buying the manufactured stuff, it hasn't got all kinds of preservatives in it, either. Best of all, store it in an airtight container and it'll last a month—but it's so good, it'll be gone long before that. And you can eat it as a snack—not just for breakfast.

INGREDIENTS
4 cups rolled oats
1 cup sliced almonds
1 cup chopped pecans
1 cup raw sunflower
    seeds or pumpkin
    seeds

⅓ cup melted butter
½ cup honey
1 teaspoon vanilla extract
1 tablespoon ground cinnamon

Preheat oven to 300°. In a large bowl, stir the oats, nuts, and sunflower kernels together. In a separate bowl, mix together the oil, honey, vanilla, and cinnamon. Add to the dry ingredients; mix well. Spread the mixture onto two ungreased (foil-lined) baking sheets. Bake for 10-12 minutes, remove from oven and stir. Return to the oven and continue baking until golden; about 10 minutes. (The longer you bake it, the darker and crispier it will get.) Remove from the oven and let it cool completely before storing.
Yield: 4 cups.

TOAST

Handmade lace vendor Ida Mitchell doesn't have much in the way of a culinary experience, but she asked me to include her favorite breakfast recipe.

INGREDIENTS
2 slices of bread
optional: butter, jam, jelly, peanut butter, etc.

"The evening before breakfast, take the butter (in a butter dish) from the refrigerator so it will be soft the next morning. Come morning, remove the twist tie from a store-bought loaf of bread. Take out two slices of bread. Place the bread in a toaster. Push down the toaster lever. Wait approximately 2 minutes. The toasted bread will jump into the air. Catch it. Place it on a plate. Spread softened butter from the butter dish onto the toast. Take a bite. Enjoy. You may also spread jam, jelly, or peanut butter, or squash a ripe banana on the toast for a tasty difference."
Yield: 1 serving.

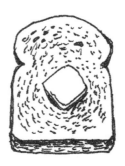

LUNCH

BLACK BEAN SOUP

I used to think nothing of opening a can of soup, heating it through, and making a nice lunch of it. Until I started growing concerned about just what was in those cans—and the disproportionate amount of sodium they contain. That's when I decided to try my hand at making my own soup. This was the first soup I ever made—and I've made it many times. The recipe doubles well, too, and you can freeze it. (Since I live alone . . . well, for right now, at least . . . I freeze it in single serving containers.)

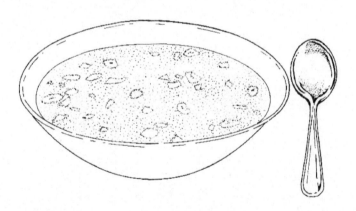

INGREDIENTS
1 cup dried black beans
1 quart cold water
½ onion, sliced
1 stalk celery, diced
2 tablespoons butter
¼ teaspoon salt
⅛ teaspoon celery salt

¼ teaspoon dry mustard
dash of red pepper flakes
2 teaspoons all-purpose flour

Wash and soak the beans overnight in cold water. Sauté the onion and celery in 1 tablespoon butter until lightly browned; add to the beans, bring to a boil and simmer, covered, for 3 hours, or until the beans are soft, adding more water as it boils away. Place the beans in a blender or food processor and blend until smooth. Return to the saucepan and reheat. Add the well-mixed seasonings. Melt the remaining 1 table-spoon of butter and stir in the flour. Gradually add the blended soup mixture and cook 3 minutes, stirring constantly until smooth and thickened.
Yield: 4 servings.

CORN CHOWDER

There's something comforting about soup or chowder on a cold day. We have the best sweet corn in the country right here in Western New York (no arguments—you cannot sway me), and this is a great way to use it. This recipe came to me from my dear friend and real estate agent Fred Cunningham. He makes it for his whole family for their yearly Labor Day get-togethers. (Yup, it always seems to be cold and rainy on Labor Day where we live.)

INGREDIENTS
1 cup chopped onion
½ cup chopped celery
2 tablespoons butter, melted
3 cups frozen corn, thawed (fresh if seasonably available)
1 ½ cups peeled, cubed potatoes
1 ½ cups water
2 chicken-flavored bouillon cubes
½ teaspoon salt
¼ teaspoon pepper
¼ teaspoon dried whole thyme
2 cups milk
1 cup half-and-half

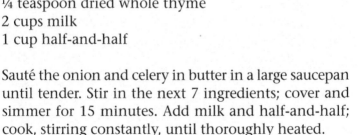

Sauté the onion and celery in butter in a large saucepan until tender. Stir in the next 7 ingredients; cover and simmer for 15 minutes. Add milk and half-and-half; cook, stirring constantly, until thoroughly heated. Yield: 8 cups.

CREAMY RED PEPPER SOUP

Artisans Alley's resident weaver, Gwen Hardy, is not only a wiz at the loom, she's a wiz in the kitchen, too. This is a soup she serves her family on a regular basis. She said she often buys a loaf of Italian bread and makes a meal of it. I've done the same. (Yum!)

INGREDIENTS
2 large onions, chopped
4 garlic cloves, minced
¼ cup butter
2 large potatoes, peels and diced
2 jars (7 ounces each) roasted red peppers, drained, patted dry and chopped
5 cups chicken broth
2 cans (15 ounces each) pears in juice
⅛ teaspoon cayenne pepper
⅛ teaspoon black pepper

In a Dutch oven, sauté the onions and garlic in butter until tender. Add the potatoes, red peppers, and broth. Bring to a boil. Reduce heat; cover and simmer for 15-20 minutes or until the vegetables are tender. Remove from the heat. Add the pears; let cool. In a blender, cover and puree in batches. Return to the pan. Stir in cayenne and black pepper. Cook until heated through.
Yield: 12 servings (approximately 3 quarts)

CORNISH PASTIES

Not all Scots are fans of their neighbors to the south, but my aunt Lizzie never held a grudge . . . well, not many, at least. And something I still love to eat for lunch on a cold day (and sometimes even in summer) is Cornish Pasties. My aunt made hers with turnips, but you can substitute carrots if you like. If you're pressed for time, ready-made pie crust works well.

PASTRY
2 cups all-purpose flour
a pinch of salt
6 tablespoons shortening
cold water
1 egg, beaten (optional)

FILLING
½ pound boneless top
    round steak chopped into
    ½ inch cubes
2 large potatoes, peeled and diced
1 large onion, chopped fine
1 medium turnip, or 2 carrots, peeled and diced
½ teaspoon salt
¼ teaspoon pepper

Preheat oven to 425°. To make the pastry, sift the flour and salt into a bowl; with a fork, mix in the shortening and add enough cold water to make a stiff dough. Mix the chopped vegetables together and sprinkle with salt and pepper. Roll the pastry out into 2 large circles. Place half the vegetables on one half of each circle and put the meat on top. Dampen the edges of the pastry and fold them over, pressing the edges together well. With a knife, cut slits in the pastry to let steam escape. Put the pasties on a baking sheet and bake for 20 minutes. (At this point, you can brush on the beaten egg.) Reduce the oven temperature to 350° and bake for 60 minutes or until golden brown. Yield: 2 servings.

DEL'S REUBEN SANDWICHES FOR SIX

As I mentioned, Seth Landers and I often meet for lunch. We'll sometimes have Chinese take-away at our office desks, but most of the time we just end up at Del's Diner, where the food is fast and fine, and the waitresses call you honey. I used to be content with just a grilled cheese sandwich and a cup of tomato soup, but my lunchtime repertoire has expanded with Seth as my tablemate, and I've grown to love Del's Reuben sandwiches. Here's the recipe he gave me. Of course, as it's from a diner, there's enough here to feed a crowd.

INGREDIENTS
⅓ cup Thousand Island salad dressing
1 tablespoon chili sauce
12 slices of rye bread, toasted
1 pound cooked corned beef, thinly sliced
1 (approximately 22-ounces) package refrigerated
     sauerkraut
6 ounces of Swiss cheese, thinly sliced

Preheat broiler. Mix the Thousand Island salad dressing with the chili sauce. Spread on the toasted rye bread. Arrange the corned beef, sauerkraut, and cheese on top of half the rye bread. Place on a baking sheet and broil 5 inches from the heat until the cheese is melted and bubbling, about 4 minutes. Top with the remaining bread and serve immediately.
Yield: 6 servings.

GRILLED CHEESE SANDWICH

How can you talk about lunch and not mention grilled cheese sandwiches? I must admit, until I moved over Andy's pizza shop on Victoria Square, I was rarely home at lunchtime to make them, but now that I'm in my new digs I can run over to my apartment and make a quick lunch—for me and for Andy. On a cold day, we like to have a warming bowl of tomato soup on the side.

The beauty of grilled cheese is that you can make it every day of the week and by changing the variety of cheese, make a totally different sandwich. When I'm in a hurry, I just use American cheese slices, but if I have a chance to go to the deli I'll pick up cheddar, mozzarella, Monterey Jack, or provolone. And Andy grows his own tomatoes behind the pizzeria so in summer he lets me take what I want. I love to put a slice of tomato or ham on the sandwich as well.

This version is for one sandwich, but it can be easily recalculated to make two, three or more. By the way, if you don't have a grill plate on your stove—no problem! A skillet will do just fine.

Ingredients

2 slices of sliced white bread (or whatever bread
    pleases you)
2 deli slices of cheddar cheese
butter (room temperature)
cooking spray

Spray the unheated surface of a skillet with cooking spray and place it on the stove burner on medium heat. Spread butter on one side of each slice of bread. When the skillet is hot, place the first slice of buttered bread inside. Place the cheese slices on the bread and top with the unbuttered side of the other slice of bread touching the cheese. Cook, pressing down gently on each sandwich with a spatula 3 or 4 times until golden and slightly crusty on the first side (3-4 minutes). Turn the sandwich and continue cooking, again pressing down on them until the second side is gold and the cheese has begun to ooze out the sides slightly, 2-3 minutes longer. Transfer to your plate and serve immediately. (And what goes best with a grilled cheese sandwhich? Potato chips! You'll feel like you're at Del's Diner.)
Yield: 1 sandwich.

MACARONI AND CHEESE

My late husband Chad was a huge fan of this dish. I swear, if I didn't complain he would have eaten it five or six days a week. Usually he was content to make the kind from a box, but for what he deemed "special occasions" he'd make it from scratch. I didn't mind eating that version, which I'm happy to share with you here.

FOR THE MACARONI
INGREDIENTS
½ teaspoon salt
2 ½ cups dried elbow macaroni (or whatever kind of pasta you prefer)
1 tablespoon vegetable or olive oil

FOR THE SAUCE
INGREDIENTS
3 tablespoons butter
3 tablespoons all-purpose flour
2 ½ cups milk, warmed
1 ¾ cups shredded sharp cheddar cheese
¼ teaspoon salt
½ teaspoon freshly ground pepper
2 teaspoons prepared Dijon-style mustard

FOR THE TOPPING
¾ cup shredded sharp cheddar cheese
½ cup fresh bread crumbs (or Panko crumbs)
1 teaspoon butter, cut into small pieces

Preheat the oven to 375°. Grease (butter or use cooking spray) an 8 x 8 x 2-inch square baking pan.

For the macaroni: bring a large pot of water (three-fourths full) to a rapid boil. Add the salt and the macaroni. Cook, stirring occasionally until al dente (5-7 minutes), or according the package instructions. Drain and rinse with cool water to remove excess starch. Place in a large mixing bowl and drizzle with the oil.

For the sauce: in a saucepan (over medium heat), melt the butter. Sprinkle the flour over the butter and whisk constantly until the flour is absorbed and the mixture is gently bubbling and a light gold in color (2-3 minutes). Gradually add the warm milk, whisking constantly. Bring to a simmer. Continue to simmer and stir until smooth and slightly thickened.

Add the 1 ¾ cups of cheese to the milk mixture, remove from the heat and whisk constantly until the cheese melts. Stir in the salt, pepper, and mustard. Pour the sauce over the macaroni and mix to combine. Transfer the macaroni to the prepared baking pan.

Bake until the top bubbles and begins to form a crust (20-25 minutes). Cover the pan with aluminum foil if it begins to brown too much. Remove from the oven and let stand for about 5 minutes before serving. Yield: 4 servings. (Well, the two of us always ate the whole thing in one sitting.)

PELICAN'S NEST TOMATO LEEK TART

McKinlay Mill's lawyer, Seth Landers, and I make time to have lunch together at least once a week. Not long ago he took me to Thompson's Landing where the new marina has brought back McKinlay Mill's waterfront. We dined alfresco at The Pelican's Nest. We both chose their Tomato Leek Tart. It was divine! I asked for and got the recipe. Of course, I always make my own pastry crust, but if you're strapped for time, you can substitute store pie crust (and that's the way I've presented this recipe). It's great for dinner, too.

INGREDIENTS
1 package refrigerated pie pastry (enough for 2 crusts)
1 cup (4 ounces) shredded provolone cheese
1 pound leeks (white portion only), sliced
6 medium plum tomatoes, thinly sliced
½ cup grated Parmesan cheese
1 ½ teaspoons garlic powder
⅛ teaspoon pepper
1 cup (8 ounces) shredded mozzarella cheese

Preheat oven to 425°. Place both pastry sheets on greased baking sheets. Sprinkle each with provolone cheese, leaving 1 inch around the edges. Arrange leeks and tomato slices over provolone cheese. Sprinkle with Parmesan cheese, garlic powder and pepper. Top with mozzarella cheese. Fold the edges over the filling. Bake for 18-22 minutes or until the crusts are lightly browned. Cut into wedges. Serve warm.
Yield: 2 tarts.

ZUCCHINI QUICHE

One of the first places Chad took me for a lunch date was a lovely little restaurant overlooking the Erie Canal. The luncheon special was zucchini quiche. It was delicious and I was determined to figure out the recipe for myself. Here's what I came up with.

INGREDIENTS
1 small (8-inch) zucchini
6 eggs
1 medium onion, chopped
1 medium green pepper, chopped
1 medium red pepper, chopped
1 tablespoon olive oil (or other cooking oil)
1 cup shredded Swiss cheese
½ teaspoon dried basil
½ teaspoon garlic powder
¼ teaspoon black pepper
cooking spray

Preheat oven to 350° Chop the onion and peppers into bite-sized pieces. In a large skillet, over medium heat, sauté the onions and peppers in the oil. Mix all the ingredients in a large bowl and pour into a 9 x 9 inch pie pan that has been prepared with cooking spray. Bake for 40 minutes or until golden brown. Let stand for 10 minutes before serving. (It's not bad served cold, either.)
Yield: 4-6 servings.

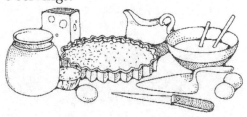

ḤORS D'OEUVRES

BACON-WRAPPED APRICOTS

For some reason I always think about the holidays when I eat these wonderful little bit-sized treats. Maybe because the first time I had them was at a New Year's Eve party some years back. Sadly, I don't remember who gave me the recipe, but I wish I did so I could thank her.

Ingredients
1 package (14 ounces) dried apricots
½ cup whole almonds
1 pound sliced bacon
¼ cup apple jelly
2 tablespoons salt-reduced soy sauce

Preheat oven to 375°. Fold each apricot around an almond. Cut bacon strips into thirds. Wrap a strip around each apricot and secure it with a toothpick. Place on two foil-lined ungreased baking trays. Bake, uncovered, for 25 minutes or until the bacon is crisp, turning once.

In a small saucepan, combine the jelly and soy sauce and cook and stir over low heat for 5 minutes. Remove apricots from the baking pan and set on paper towels to drain. Serve with the sauce for dipping.
Yield: Approximately 4 ½ dozen.

CURRIED DEVILED EGGS

One of the easiest finger foods you can make is deviled eggs, and they're so versatile, too. You can change
the spices or other ingredients for a different taste.
(Sometimes I make mine with horseradish flavored
mayonnaise. Yummy!) But my favorite are curried
deviled eggs. I like a strong curry flavor, but you can
decrease the amount of curry powder if you so desire.

INGREDIENTS
4 hard boiled eggs
⅓ cup mayonnaise
1 teaspoon curry powder
1 teaspoon prepared yellow mustard
paprika (optional)

Hard boil the eggs and let them cool. Peel and slice
the eggs length wise. Scoop out the yolks and place
them in a small bowl. Mash the yolks with a fork. Stir
in mayonnaise, curry powder, and mustard until
smooth and creamy. Spoon or pipe the mixture into
the egg white halves. If desired, sprinkle with paprika.
Refrigerate 1 hour or until ready to serve.
Yield: 4 servings (2 halves each).

RYE BOAT

For some reason, this great dip tastes best while watching a football game. (Here in Western New York, we watch the Buffalo Bills. Sometimes they even win!)

INGREDIENTS
1 ⅓ cups sour cream
1 ⅓ cups mayonnaise
2 tablespoons dried onion
2 tablespoons dried parsley
2 tablespoons dried dill weed
1 5-ounce jar of dried beef
2 large loaves of unsliced (round) rye bread (seeded or unseeded)

Cut out the center of one of the rye loaves, saving the pieces to use for dipping. Cut the dried beef into thin slices. (Kitchen scissors work just as well.) In a medium-sized bowl, combine all the other ingredients and the beef and mix well. Transfer the dip to the middle of the hollowed-out loaf. Cut the second rye loaf into 1-inch pieces. (If you make the dip in advance, wait until ready to serve to put it in the bread boat.) Yield: 1 ⅔ cups.

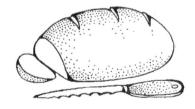

SUN-DRIED TOMATO DIP

Nothing tastes as magical as sun-dried tomtoes. I love them with pasta, on a sandwich, and even in a bagel. This is one of my favorite dips, and maybe it'll be yours, too.

INGREDIENTS
1 8-ounce package cream cheese, softened
½ cup sour cream
½ cup mayonnaise
1 jar (8 ounces) sun-dried tomatoes, drained and
    chopped (about ½ cup)
¾ teaspoon salt
½ teaspoon ground black pepper
¼ - ½ teaspoon bottled hot pepper sauce
2 green onions, sliced
milk (optional)

In a food processor bowl or blender container, combine the cream cheese, sour cream, mayonnaise, dried tomatoes, salt, pepper and bottle hot pepper sauce. Cover and process or blend until almost smooth. Add the green onions. Cover and process or blend until the onion is coarsely chopped. Cover and refrigerate. Remove the dip from the refrigerator 20 minutes before serving. If desired, stir in a little milk to thin to dipping consistency. Serve with assorted fresh vegetables, crackers, or potato chips.
Yield: 2 ½ cups.

SPINACH BALLS

During the past year, Seth Landers has hosted several gatherings for business associates and friends at his lovely old farmhouse. I've been lucky enough to be invited to these soirees and even helped him prepare a few of the appetizers in his fabulous kitchen. These lovely little spinach bites are tasty, and I've decided that since they contain ingredients from several food groups they must be good for you, too. (That's my story and I'm sticking to it.)

INGREDIENTS
2 (10 ounce) packages chopped spinach, thawed and
    squeezed dry
4 eggs
2 cups seasoned breadcrumbs
1 large onion, chopped
1 cup grated Swiss cheese
½ cup grated parmesan cheese
¼ teaspoon powdered garlic
¼ teaspoon salt

Mix ingredients together. Chill 1 hour. Preheat oven to 350°. Form the spinach mixture into balls and bake for 15 to 20 minutes. Serve hot.
Yield: 3 dozen.

STUFFED MUSHROOMS FLORENTINE

Detective Ray Davenport, of the Monroe County Sheriff's Office, and I did not start out on great terms. But because of the deaths that have occurred on Victoria Square, he seems to hang round the place quite a lot. I must have been feeling particularly generous the day I asked him for a recipe for this book. I thought he'd growl at me, but instead he said he'd love to . . . with one caveat. He doesn't cook. But he said his daughter Sophie had a great recipe for stuffed mushrooms that he thought I might like. Did I ever! I hope you'll like them, too.

INGREDIENTS
24 large fresh mushrooms
1 (10-ounce) package of
   frozen leaf spinach
1 clove garlic, minced
½ cup butter
1 small onion, finely
   chopped
2 (3-ounce) packages
   cream cheese, soft-
   ened
½ cup fine, dry bread-
   crumbs
⅛ teaspoon pepper
¾ teaspoon dry mustard
¼ teaspoon ground nutmeg
2 ½ tablespoons grated Parmesan cheese

Preheat oven to 375°. Clean the mushrooms with a damp paper towel. Remove the stems and chop; set aside. Cook the spinach according to the package directions, omitting the salt. Drain well. Place spinach in a blender or food processor and process until smooth. Set aside. Sauté the garlic in butter in a skillet over low hear for one minute. Dip the mushroom caps in the butter garlic mixture, coating well. Place them on a foil-lined baking tray. Stir the chopped mushroom stems and onion into the remaining butter and garlic mixture and sauté until tender. Combine the spinach, cream cheese, breadcrumbs, and seasonings in a medium bowl. Add the mushroom mixture into mushroom caps and sprinkle with the Parmesan cheese. Bake for 15 minutes.

Yield: 24 mushrooms

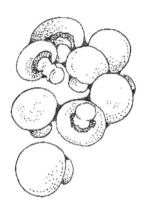

SOUTH OF THE BORDER MINI QUICHES

When Detective Davenport's daughter Sophie heard about this cookbook, she not only offered the previous recipe, but suggested I add this one, too. Sophie hopes to be a professional chef one day, so it isn't surprising she wants to share her love of food with the world—and Victoria Square—at large.

INGREDIENTS
½ cup butter or margarine, softened
1 package (3 ounces) cream cheese, softened
1 cup all-purpose flour
1 cup (4 ounces) Monterey Jack cheese
1 can (4 ounces) green chilies, drained
2 eggs
½ cup whipping cream
¼ to ½ teaspoon ground cumin
¼ teaspoon salt
⅛ teaspoon pepper

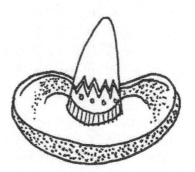

Preheat oven to 350°. In a small mixing bowl, blend butter and cream cheese. Add flour; beat until well blended. Shape into 24 balls; cover and refrigerate for 1 hour. Press balls into the bottom and the sides of greased mini muffin cups. Sprinkle a rounded teaspoon of cheese and ½ teaspoon of chilies into each shell. In a bowl, beat eggs, cream, ground cumin, salt and pepper. Spoon into shells. Bake for 30-35 minutes or until golden brown. Let stand for 5 minutes before serving. Refrigerate leftovers.
Yield: 2 dozen.

DINNER

SCALLOPS AL FORNO

As I mentioned, my late husband Chad did most of the cooking in our home, but this was something even I could make. It's pretty much goof-proof. You'll impress company or just your family with this easy-to-make dinner for two or four. I tried it on my beau Andy Rust and he loved it, too. It looked good, it smelled heavenly, and he was skeptical that I actually made it. The crunchy Panko breadcrumbs contrast nicely with the delicate flavor of the scallops. The beauty of this recipe is that it can be used with other seafood, such as cod or shrimp. The results should be similar, but some experimentation might be necessary when it comes to timing and quantities.

INGREDIENTS
1 pound fresh scallops (if frozen, thaw)
¼ cup basting or olive oil
1 cup Panko breadcrumbs
1 teaspoon garlic powder

Preheat oven to 450° using a non-stick foil on a baking tray for easy clean up. In a bowl, mix Panko crumbs with the basting oil and garlic powder until nicely saturated.* Dip each scallop into the crumb mixture and roll until covered and place on baking tray. With your hand or a spoon, spread the remaining crumbs over the scallops and pat down to coat evenly. Bake approximately 15 minutes, or until the fish reads 130° in the center and the crust is nicely browned. (*If desired, add about 2 tbsp. chopped fresh or frozen parsley to the mix.)
Yield: 2 servings.

CONRAD STRATTON'S CHICKEN WITH WINE SAUCE

Victoria Square is the home to The Perfect Grape wine shop, owned by Conrad Stratton. In addition to his knowledge of fine wines, Conrad is also a gourmet and loves to cook. He gave me this recipe and it's so easy to make that I've already made it several times. You'll want to add it to your regular dinner repertoire.

INGREDIENTS
4 skinless, boneless chicken breast halves cut into
    strips
2 eggs, beaten
½ cup Parmesan cheese
1 pinch sea salt
1 pinch ground black pepper
½ cup white wine
4 tablespoons butter

Season the chicken with salt and pepper to taste. In a shallow plate, spread Parmesan cheese. Divide chicken into three parts and dip seasoned chicken in eggs, then coat well with Parmesan cheese. Repeat until all of the chicken pieces are well coated (if you run short on egg and Parmesan, add one more egg and more Parmesan as needed).

In a skillet, melt butter or margarine over medium high heat. Cook chicken, stirring frequently, until golden brown.

Reduce the heat and add the wine. Cover and simmer over low heat for 20 minutes.

Serve over white rice or pasta.

Yield: 4 servings.

CABBAGE CASSEROLE

This is an easy-peasy recipe that doesn't take long to whip up and is easy on the calories, too. Makes great leftovers.

INGREDIENTS
1 16-ounce smoked turkey
    sausage, cut into coins
3 cups shredded cabbage
½ cup onion, chopped
1 medium apple, cored and
    chopped.
cooking spray

Spray a large skillet with cooking spray. Add the sausage, cabbage, onion, and apple. Cover and simmer on medium heat for about 20 minutes.
Yield: 4-5 servings.

EASY PESTO

Along with the tomatoes, Andy Rust also grows herbs in his garden. He lets me take what I want and I love making this pesto from scratch. It's delish!

INGREDIENTS
¼ cup Chicken Broth
¼ cup olive oil
1 cup packed fresh basil leaves
2 cloves garlic, minced
¼ cup grated Parmesan cheese
4 cups hot cooked spaghetti, cooked without salt

Place broth, basil, garlic and cheese in a blender or food processor. Cover and blend until smooth. Toss with spaghetti. Goes great with a fresh salad and Italian bread.
Yield: 4 servings.

DEL'S MEATLOAF

Nobody makes meatloaf like my great-aunt Lizzie did, but the meatloaf at Del's Diner comes close. It's Seth Landers' favorite meal. I twisted Del's arm and he shared his recipe with me.

INGREDIENTS
1 ½ pounds lean ground beef
⅔ cup seasoned breadcrumbs
1 egg, beaten
1 medium onion, chopped
¼ teaspoon salt
¼ teaspoon ground pepper
⅔ cup ketchup
1 tablespoon Worcestershire sauce

Preheat oven to 350°. Combine the breadcrumbs, egg, onion, salt and pepper, and mix well. Add to ground beef and mix well. Shape mixture into a loaf shape in baking dish or tray. Mix ketchup with Worcestershire sauce and pour over the top. Bake for 70-80 minutes (or until meat thermometer reads 160°).
Yield: 4-6 servings.

EASY CRAB CAKES

My friend (and erstwhile big brother) Seth Landers is a busy attorney by day, and an accomplished host by  night. He's got a kitchen to die for, and often entertains friends for dinner. One of his specialties is crab cakes. He's made them for me more than once, and I love them. You will, too.

INGREDIENTS
2 cans (6 ounces each) crabmeat, drained
1 cup seasoned bread crumbs (divided)
1 egg, slightly beaten
½ cup finely chopped green onions
¼ cup mayonnaise
1 tablespoon lemon juice
½ teaspoon garlic powder
⅛ teaspoon red pepper flakes
1 tablespoon butter

In a large bowl, combine the crab, ⅓ cup bread crumbs, egg, onions, mayonnaise, lemon juice, garlic powder and red pepper flakes. Divide the mixture into eight portions. Shape into 2-inch balls. Roll in the remaining bread crumbs. Flatten into ½-inch thickness. In a large skillet, cook the crab cakes in butter for 3 to 4 minutes on each side or until golden brown.
Yield: 4 servings

EDIE SILVER'S SOUTHWEST CHICKEN STEW

Edie Silver is a marvel. Not only does she make beautiful silk flower arrangements, and other hand-crafted items (she crochets, she knits, she sews—is there any craft she can't handle?), but she volunteers to work at every special event held at Artisans Alley. She also loves to cook for her large family. (She has three kids and six grandchildren!) This recipe is one of their favorites.

INGREDIENTS

1 ½ pounds boneless chicken breasts or thighs cut into ¾-inch pieces
1 tablespoon chili powder
1 teaspoon ground cumin
¾ teaspoon salt
1 red bell pepper, cut into ¾-inch pieces
1 green bell pepper, cut into ¾-inch pieces
1 medium onion (red or yellow), chopped
3 cloves garlic, minced
1 can (15 ½ ounces) chili beans in spicy sauce, undrained
1 can (14 ½ ounces) chili style stewed tomatoes, undrained
¾ cup prepared salsa or picante sauce
fresh cilantro (optional)

Place the chicken in a slow cooker. Sprinkle chili powder, cumin, and salt over the chicken. Toss to coat. Add peppers, onion, garlic, beans, tomatoes, and salsa. Mix well. Cover and cook on low for 5 hours or

until the chicken is no longer pink in the center and the vegetables are crisp-tender. Ladle into bowls. If desired, garnish with cilantro.
Yield: 4-6 servings.

GILDA RINGWALD-STRATTON'S SLOW COOKER BRISKET

One of my favorite shops on Victoria Square is Gilda's Gourmet Baskets. Gilda has a knack for putting together gift baskets that sooth your soul or brighten your day, and she makes them for every occasion imaginable. All that takes time, so it's no wonder she relies on her faithful slow cooker to turn out meals that taste like she fussed for hours.

INGREDIENTS
4 pounds fresh beef brisket
2 teaspoons salt
2 teaspoons dry mustard
2 teaspoons paprika
⅛ teaspoon pepper
½ teaspoon garlic powder

Trim all excess fat from the brisket. Combine seasonings until well blended; rub into brisket. Place the meat in a slow cooker with fat side up, cutting to fit if necessary. Cover and cook on low for 8 to 12 hours. Remove the brisket from the liquid and cut across the grain into thin slices. Serve with the juices.
Yield: 4-6 servings (or see below).

What should you do with the leftover brisket? Make beef barbeque, of course! The leftover brisket should be almost totally loose, like pulled pork (i.e. no longer in slices). Store in the refrigerator until ready for the following recipe.

GILDA'S BEEF BARBECUE

In a medium bowl, add the following:
1½ cups water
2 cups ketchup
½ cup cider vinegar
¼ cup Worcestershire Sauce
¾ cup light brown sugar

Stir until the brown sugar and other ingredients are well dissolved. Add to a bowlful of your precooked brisket and mix well, separating the meat evenly. Put in a saucepan on low heat, just to warm through, for about ½ to ¾ hour, the last 15 minutes you can turn it down to your lowest setting ("warm" on most electric stoves). To serve, remove from the heat and spoon onto hamburger buns.
Yield: 2-4 servings.

SLOW COOKER BAKED BEANS

I know, I know—how can you bake beans in a slow cooker? Well, trust me, this recipe works and is delicious. And, as with most slow cooker recipes, there's not a lot of effort involved. They're great for potluck dinners, too.

INGREDIENTS
1 pound dried navy beans (about 2 ¼ cups)
1 ½ cup chopped onion
5 cups water
½ cup ketchup
⅓ cup molasses
⅓ cup brown sugar, packed
1 teaspoon dry mustard
¾ teaspoon salt
¼ teaspoon pepper

Combine the beans, onion, and water in 3 ½ quart slow cooker. Stir. Cover. Cook on low for 8 to 10 hours or on high for 4 to 5 hours. Add remaining 6 ingredients. Stir well. Cook on high for about 30 minutes to blend flavors.
Yield: 6 servings.

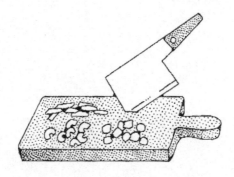

SLOW COOKED BEEF

When I was in grad school, I never had time to cook. My husband, Chad, was just as busy working full time as an English teacher at McKinlay Mill High and spending his off hours at Artisans Alley. It was Chad who made most of our dinners in those days, and he often started our meals in the slow cooker before he went to work.

INGREDIENTS

1 pound round steak or roast
1 can stewed tomatoes
1 tablespoon of brown sugar
1 - 1 ½ teaspoon dried mustard
2 teaspoon Worcestershire sauce
1 medium onions, chopped
1 medium green pepper, chopped

Turn on slow cooker to low. In a small bowl, mix tomatoes, sugar, mustard and Worcestershire sauce. Place meat on the bottom of the cooker. Cover with onions and peppers. Pour the liquid ingredients over the meat and vegetables. Cook for 7 to 9 hours. Serve over cooked rice or noodles.
Yield: 4 servings.

SLOW COOKER CHILI

Dennis Wheeler owns the wood and gift shop, Wood U, on Victoria Square. During the school year, he's the Industrial Arts instructor at McKinlay Mill High School. "Cook? Me?" he said when I mentioned this cookbook to him one Saturday at his shop. Luckily his wife, Abby, who runs the shop while Dennis is at school, stepped up to the plate. "Since we both work almost seven days a week, who has time to cook? I make a lot of our meals in the slow cooker. This recipe is one of Dennis's favorites."

INGREDIENTS
1 pound ground beef
2 cans (16 ounces each) kidney beans, rinsed and
    drained
1 can (14 ounces) stewed tomatoes, undrained
1 can (4 ounces) chopped green chilies
2-3 teaspoons chili powder
1 teaspoon cumin powder
½ teaspoon dried basil
¼ teaspoon salt
⅛ teaspoon pepper

In a large skillet, cook the beef over medium heat until no longer pink. Transfer to a 3 quart slow cooker. Stir in the remaining ingredients. Cover and cook on low for up to six hours.
Yield: 6 servings.

KIELBASA WITH BEANS

For a while there, Janey Ingram was quite ill. Thankfully she is in remission and is once again her smiling self. But while she was under the weather, Vance literally stepped up to the plate and did the majority of the cooking for Janey and their son, Vance Junior. This recipe doesn't take a lot of ingredients or a lot of time, and it sure tastes good.

INGREDIENTS
½ pound sliced bacon
1 pound smoked kielbasa or turkey sausage, cut into coins
1 large onion, chopped
1 medium green pepper, chopped
2 cans kidney beans, rinsed and drained
½ cup chicken broth
pepper to taste

In a large skillet, cook the bacon until crisp. Remove to a paper towel to drain. Discard all but 1 tablespoon of the bacon drippings. Cook the kielbasa in drippings until lightly browned. Drain. Add the onion, pepper, beans, broth and pepper. Cover and simmer for 1 hour, stirring occasionally. Crumble the bacon on top.
Yield: 4-6 servings

ORANGE-GLAZED CHICKEN

Being a Scot, my aunt Lizzie loved marmalade. (I think it's almost a prerequisite.) This was a recipe she found in a magazine many years ago and she would make it at least once a month. She never tired of it and neither did I.

INGREDIENTS
2 tablespoons all-purpose flour
½ teaspoon salt (optional)
½ teaspoon pepper
2 boneless skinless chicken breast halves
3 teaspoons vegetable oil
1 teaspoon orange marmalade
1 cup orange juice
dash of ground nutmeg

Combine the flour, salt (if desired) and pepper. Coat each chicken breast. In a skillet, heat the oil on medium. Brown the chicken. Spread the marmalade on top of the chicken; sprinkle with the nutmeg. Add the orange juice and simmer 10-15 minutes or until the chicken juices run clear. (Can easily be doubled to serve 4.) Yield: 2 servings.

PARMESAN CHICKEN

Want something easy to make that doesn't take long in the oven, and tastes terrific? You can't go wrong with this recipe, which I got from Edie Silver. She says it's foolproof. She often makes a half size version, or doubles it depending on whether it's just her and her husband for dinner, or she invites the whole gang.

INGREDIENTS
4 boneless skinless chicken breast halves (1 pound)
½ cup mayonnaise
½ cup grated parmesan cheese
1 teaspoon dried oregano
¼ teaspoon pepper
paprika, optional
cooking spray

Preheat oven to 400°. Place the chicken in a shallow baking dish that has been coated with cooking spray. Bake, uncovered, for 20 minutes. Combine the mayonnaise, cheese, oregano, and pepper. Spread the mixture over the chicken. Sprinkle with paprika if desired. Bake 20 minutes more or until the chicken juices run clear.
Yield: 4 servings.

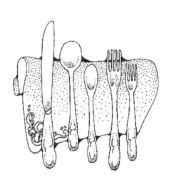

SAUSAGE AND BARLEY STUFFED PEPPERS

When autumn comes it's time to shift gears and think about comfort food. Rose Nash invited me for dinner just after I became manager of Artisans Alley and served this very different twist on traditional stuffed peppers. She told me it was her late husband Howard's favorite dish. I can see why.

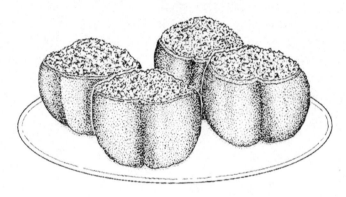

INGREDIENTS
1 cup chicken broth
4 medium bell peppers, any color, with tops removed and seeded (reserve tops)
1 pound pork (or turkey) sausage (mild or spicy-- your choice)
1 medium onion, chopped
3 garlic cloves, minced
1 cup cooked pearl barley
1 cup chunky salsa
¼ teaspoon ground cumin
salt and pepper to taste
1 cup shredded mozzarella cheese, divided
sour cream (optional)

Preheat oven to 350°. Par-boil the peppers for 3 to 5 minutes in salted water. Pour the chicken broth into a 9 x 13 inch baking dish and set aside. In a large skillet, cook the sausage, onion, chopped pepper tops, and garlic until the sausage is browned; drain fat if desired. Stir in barley, salsa, and cumin; Add salt and pepper to taste and mix well; add ½ cup of the shredded cheese and combine with other ingredients. Fill the peppers with the sausage/barley mixture and place in the prepared baking dish. Cover the baking dish tightly with aluminum foil and bake for 45-50 minutes. Sprinkle the rest of the cheese over the peppers and bake for another 5 minutes or until the cheese is melted. Serve with additional salsa and sour cream as topping.

Yield: 4 servings.

VANCE INGRAM'S BARBEQUED RIBS

Vance told me, "Unlike my wife, I didn't come from the south where men are often judged on their barbeque prowess. But over the years I developed this sweet-and-sour sauce that's not only easy to make, but it tastes damn fine. We like our ribs blackened, and the brown sugar in this recipe does the trick."

INGREDIENTS
⅔ cup ketchup
1 teaspoon prepared yellow mustard
4 tablespoons brown sugar (packed)
2 dashes of Worcestershire sauce
2 teaspoons red wine vinegar
1 rack of pork ribs

In a small bowl, mix the ketchup, mustard, sugar, Worcestershire sauce and vinegar until blended well. Set aside. Light the barbeque grill. When the grill is hot, put the ribs on. When they're about halfway cooked (about ten minutes), use a pastry brush to add the sauce to the ribs. Place the sauce side on the heated surface. Cook for 5 or more minutes. Turn over. Brush sauce on the other side. Repeat as needed. Yield: 2 or 3 or 4 servings. (That depends on how much you like ribs. You don't have to share.)

SIDE DISHES

APRICOT CARROTS

My aunt Lizzie loved both carrots and apricots, so it's not surprising that she came up with this dish which we often had with roast beef or chicken.

INGREDIENTS
1 pound carrots, sliced in
    coins
¼ cup apricot preserves
1 tablespoon butter
1 teaspoon lemon juice
¼ teaspoon grated orange peel
⅛ teaspoon ground nutmeg

Place the carrots in a saucepan with enough water to cover. Bring to a boil. Cover and cook for 8-10 minutes or until they are crisp-tender. Drain. Add remaining ingredients. Cover and stir over medium heat for 3 minutes or until the preserves are melted and the carrots are coated.
Yield: 4 servings.

PARSNIP CAKES

When I was growing up, I doubt any of my classmates even knew what a parsnip was. Aha, I thought, more for me! What a wonderful vegetable. Only—it's sweet. And it's versatile. But my favorite way of cooking (and then eating) parsnips is these golden "cakes." They go well with dinner (and I've been known to reheat them in the microwave and eat them for breakfast, too).

INGREDIENTS
2 pounds boiled and mashed parsnips
1 cup all-purpose flour
2 eggs, lightly beaten
½ cup dry breadcrumbs (or cornmeal)
¼ teaspoon salt
¼ teaspoon freshly ground pepper
4 tablespoons butter, melted
oil for frying.

Measure and mix the flour, salt, and pepper. Mix the parsnips with half the flour mixture. Add the butter and knead the mixture into a dough. Form it into round flat cakes, dust them with the remaining flour, dip them in the egg and coat them with breadcrumbs. Heat the oil and fry the parsnip cakes on both sides until golden brown. Serve immediately.
Yield: 6-8 servings.

ANDY'S PEPPERONI PASTA SALAD

Pizza isn't the only thing that Andy Rust excels at making. The Merchants Association had a potluck dinner once and Andy brought this pasta salad. Since then, I've asked him to make it several times. It's easy and it sure is tasty.

INGREDIENTS
6 ounces (tri-colored) spiral pasta
½ cup vegetable oil
½ cup red wine vinegar
¼ cup grated Parmesan cheese
1 teaspoon dried basil
1 teaspoon dried oregano
½ teaspoon salt
⅛ teaspoon dried red pepper flakes (optional)
1 cup grape tomatoes
1 red onion, thinly sliced
30-40 pepperoni slices
2 cups broccoli, cooked but firm
½ pound provolone cheese, cubed
grated mozzarella cheese

Mix oil, basil, oregano, salt, and red pepper. Add the cooked and drained (but still warm) pasta and toss with the Parmesan cheese. Cover and refrigerate for 2 hours. Add the broccoli, pepperoni, onion, cheese, and tomatoes. Mix well. Optional: sprinkle with the grated mozzarella cheese and garnish with several red onion rings.
Yield: 4-6 servings.

ROSE NASH'S POTATO SALAD

Rose Nash was the very first Artisans Alley vendor I met on a cold October day not so long ago. Since then, we've become fast friends. Rose is a widow, so she doesn't have the opportunity to do much cooking, but she pulls out all the stops when we have an Artisans Alley potluck. This is the potato salad she always brings. Hmm . . . maybe it's time to arrange another potluck, because this recipe is one of my favorites.

INGREDIENTS
6 cups diced peeled cooked potatoes
4 hard-boiled eggs
½ cup chopped celery
½ cup chopped sweet pickles
⅓ cup chopped onion
⅓ cup chopped radishes
½ cup mayonnaise
3 tablespoons sugar
1 tablespoon vinegar
1 tablespoon milk
1 ½ teaspoon prepared
   mustard
½ teaspoon salt
paprika, optional

In a large bowl, combine the potatoes, eggs, celery, pickles, onion and radishes. In another bowl, combine the mayonnaise, sugar, vinegar, milk, mustard and salt. Mix well. Pour the liquid mixture over the potato mixture and stir to coat. Cover and refrigerate. If desired, sprinkle with paprika before serving.
Yield: 6-8 servings.

SAUSAGE RICE CASSEROLE

As I mentioned earlier, my late husband Chad was a nut for casseroles. They were a treat after days and days of some of his uninspired menus. This was his favorite growing up. And while his mother always served this as a main meal, it's great as a side dish, too.

INGREDIENTS
1 cup uncooked white rice
2 cups chopped carrots
1 large onion, chopped
1 cup chopped celery
½ cup chopped green pepper
1 can (14 ½ ounce) chicken broth
¼ cup water
1 pound bulk pork or poultry sausage (mild or
    spicy—your choice)
cooking spray

Preheat oven to 350°. Lightly coat a 3-quart casserole dish with cooking spray. Spread the rice evenly on the bottom of the dish. Spoon the vegetables over the rice. Pour the chicken broth and water over the vegetables. Cook the sausage until browned; drain well. Spoon the sausage over the vegetables. Cover and bake for 30 minutes. Remove from oven and stir well. Cover and bake an additional 30 minutes.
Yield: 8-10 servings

SWEET AND SOUR GREEN BEANS

Edie Silver is a busy woman who does everything well—including cooking. She says she often whips these up on a weeknight for her husband and herself. "They're supposed to serve four to six, but they're so good sometimes we eat the whole batch," she confided to me. You might want to do the same.

INGREDIENTS
1 ¼ pounds fresh green beans
4 slices of bacon
1 small onion, chopped
¾ cup granulated sugar
½ cup vinegar

Wash and cut green beans into 1-inch pieces. (Remove any strings, first!) Set aside. Cook bacon in a large skillet until crisp. Remove bacon from skillet, and reserve drippings. Crumble the bacon and set aside. Sauté the onion in the bacon drippings until tender. Add the sugar, stirring until dissolved. Stir in bacon, beans, and vinegar. Cover and bring to a boil. Reduce the heat and simmer 25 minutes or until the beans are tender.
Yield: 4-6 servings

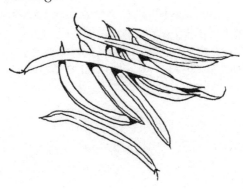

WALDORF SALAD FOR TWO

Growing up, it seemed like all my friends had large families, but I just had my great-aunt Lizzie. So I learned to make a lot of recipes for just the two of us. Waldorf Salad was something we ate for holidays: Thanksgiving, Christmas, and Easter. These days, I like to have it whenever I'm feeling in the mood to celebrate. It's a dandy reward when something good happens at Artisans Alley (like paying all the bills and still having a little leftover). Why not celebrate with some Waldorf Salad tonight? (This recipe can be easily doubled or tripled.)

INGREDIENTS
½ cup chopped, slightly toasted walnuts
½ cup celery, thinly sliced
½ cup red seedless grapes, sliced (or a ¼ cup of raisins)
1 sweet apple, cored and chopped
3 tablespoons mayonnaise or plain yogurt
1 tablespoon fresh lemon juice
salt
pepper
lettuce

In a medium sized bowl, whisk together the mayonnaise and the lemon juice. Add ½ teaspoon of salt, ¼ teaspoon of fresh ground pepper. Mix in the apple, celery, grapes, and walnuts. Serve on a bed of fresh lettuce. Yield: 2 servings.

EDIE SILVER'S CHEESY MASHED POTATOES

Edie Silver was the first of the new vendors who joined Artisans Alley only days after I became its manager. Thanks to Edie, we've had a few potluck dinners at the Alley and there's one dish that has to be there or I'm sure the vendors would stage a riot, and that's Edie's cheesy mashed potatoes. At the vendors' request, I've included the recipe for all of Victoria Square's fans. (You can double or even triple the recipe if you're going to a big gathering, and believe me, Edie does just that for our potlucks and there are never any leftovers.)

INGREDIENTS
6 large potatoes, peeled and quartered
1 packages (8 ounces) cream cheese, softened
1 cup (4 ounces) shredded cheddar cheese
½ cup sour cream
⅓ cup chopped onion
1 egg
1 teaspoon salt
½ teaspoon pepper
additional shredded cheddar cheese, optional

Place potatoes in a large saucepan; cover with water. Cover and bring to a boil. Cook for 20-25 minutes or until very tender; drain well. In a mixing bowl, mash potatoes (or whip them with a hand mixer). Add cream cheese, cheddar cheese, sour cream, onion, egg, salt and pepper; beat until fluffy. Transfer to a greased 2-quart baking dish. Cover and bake at 350° for 40-45 minutes or until heated through. If desired, sprinkle with additional cheese and bake for another 10 minutes.
Yield: 10 servings.

CORN BREAD

As I've mentioned more than once, baking equals comfort for me, and is there anything more comforting than something warm from the oven? For some reason, I like to have a hot mug of cocoa handy when this corn bread recipe comes out of the oven. But it's terrific as a side with your favorite Mexican dish, stuffed peppers, barbecue, your favorite soup, etc. (Just writing this makes me want to turn on the oven and start a batch right now.)

INGREDIENTS
1 cup yellow cornmeal
1 cup all-purpose flour
1 teaspoon salt
1 tablespoon baking powder
1 cup milk (even fat-free works)
2 tablespoons honey
2 eggs, well beaten
⅓ cup butter, melted and cooled
½ cup corn kernels (fresh or thawed frozen)

Preheat the oven to 400°. Prepare (with butter or spray oil) an 8 x 8 x 2-inch square baking pan. In a large bowl, mix together the cornmeal, flour, salt, and baking powder. In a large measuring cup, whisk together the milk, honey, and eggs. Stir the egg mixture into the cornmeal mixture. Stir in the melted butter and then gently fold in the corn kernels. Pour the batter into the prepared pan. Bake until the center is firm to the touch (18-20 minutes) Cut into squares and serve hot.
Yield: 4-6 servings.

HONEY MUSTARD SALAD DRESSING

When putting this cookbook together, I learned a lot about my friends on Victoria Square and McKinlay Mill. It turns out that Luther Collier, the owner of Collier's Funeral Home, is a vegetarian. He says he eats a lot of pulses (beans) and salads. This is his favorite salad dressing recipe.

INGREDIENTS
¼ cup buttermilk
¼ cup sour cream
2 tablespoons Dijon mustard
2 tablespoons honey
1 ½ teaspoons dried minced onion
1 teaspoons dried parley flakes

In a small bowl, whisk together all the ingredients. Serve over a tossed salad.
Yield: ½ cup.

POPPY SEED SALAD DRESSING

This dressing is another of Luther Collier's favorites. He much prefers it to the commercial products available for sale at the local grocery store. I tried it—and I think he's right!

INGREDIENTS
¾ cup granulated sugar
⅓ cup cider vinegar
4 ½ teaspoons grated onion
3 teaspoons ground mustard
1 teaspoon poppy seeds
¼ teaspoon salt
1 cup vegetable oil

In a small bowl, combine the first six ingredients. Slowly add the oil and whisk briskly. Cover and refrigerate until serving.
Yield: Makes 1 ⅓ cups.

MIGHTY-FINE BISCUITS

Janey Ingram is just a down-home girl, and one thing
that down-home girl learned to make at a tender age
was mighty-fine biscuits. She likes to say she got the
recipe from her memaw, but memaw never measured
anything. She put in a little of this and a little of that.
This is Janey's version of her memaw's biscuits.

INGREDIENTS
3 cups all-purpose flour
2 tablespoons sugar
1 tablespoon plus 1 ½ teaspoons baking powder
¾ teaspoon cream of tartar
½ teaspoon salt
¾ cup shortening
1 egg, beaten
¾ cup milk

Preheat oven to 450°. Combine the first 5 ingredients,
mixing well. Cut in the shortening with a pastry
blender until the mixture resembles coarse meal.
Combine the egg and milk. Add to the flour mixture,
stirring until the dry ingredients are moistened. Turn
the dough out onto a lightly floured surface. Knead 8
or 10 times. Roll the dough to 1-inch thickness. Cut
with 2 ½-inch biscuit cutter. Place biscuits on an ungreased, foil-lined baking sheet. Bake for 15 minutes
or until golden brown.
Yield: 15 biscuits.

VEGETARIAN SPINACH CURRY

As I mentioned, my aunt Lizzie was a curry lover. This is a recipe I know she would have loved. I've made it many times in the last year because it's filling, and not only does it taste good, it's good for you. You can eat this as a main dish or a side dish.

INGREDIENTS
1 cup chopped onion
2 garlic cloves, minced
1 tablespoon curry powder
1 tablespoon vegetable oil
1 can (8 ounces) tomato sauce
1 package (10 ounces) frozen chopped spinach,
    thawed and squeezed dry
1 can (14 ounces) garbanzo beans, rinsed and
    drained, divided
1 cup chicken or vegetable broth
¼ teaspoon salt
¼ teaspoon ground pepper

In a large skillet, cook the onion, garlic and curry powder in oil for 3-4 minutes or until the onion is tender. Stir in the tomato sauce, spinach and 1 cup of the garbanzo beans. In a blender, combine the broth and remaining garbanzo beans, cover and blend until smooth (about 2 minutes). Stir the blended mixtures into the skillet. Sprinkle with the salt and pepper. Cook and stir until the mixture is heated through. Serve over rice.
Yield: 4 servings.

DESSERTS

Children can learn a lot of life's lessons right in the kitchen, and what better way to do it than baking with a mom, a sister, a grandmother, an aunt, or some other loved one. I learned about fractions by using measuring cups and spoons. I learned that not following directions made for a failed recipe. I learned patience watching the timer count off the minutes until the cookies, pies, or cakes were baked. I learned the joy of sharing one's bounty with friends and family. For me, there is no greater joy than to bake. And what do I like to bake best? Desserts, of course!

CHOCOLATE CHIP COOKIES

If there's anyone on the face of the planet who doesn't love chocolate chip cookies, I haven't met him or her yet. I've tried many recipes in the past, and this one always works for me—and it doesn't hurt that it tastes delicious, too.

INGREDIENTS
2 ¼ cups all-purpose flour
1 teaspoon baking soda
½ teaspoon salt
1 cup (½ pound) butter, softened
¾ cup granulated sugar
¾ cup packed brown sugar
1 teaspoon vanilla extract
2 eggs
2 cups (12-ounce package) milk chocolate or semi-sweet chocolate chips
1 cup chopped walnuts (optional)

Preheat oven to 375°. Sift the flour, baking soda, and salt into a small bowl. Cream the butter, sugars, and vanilla in a large mixer bowl. Add the eggs one at a time, beating well after each addition; gradually beat in the flour mixture. Stir in the chocolate chips and nuts. Drop by rounded tablespoon onto ungreased, foil-lined baking sheets. Bake for 10-12 minutes or until golden brown. Let stand for a couple of minutes, and then remove to wire racks to cool completely. Yield: About 5 dozen cookies.

CHERRY ALMOND BAR COOKIES

One of the things I love about being a part of Victoria Square is that I get to inhale such wonderful aromas from Angelo's Pizzeria, Sweet Sue's Confectionery, Tanner's bakery, and Booth's Jellies and Jams, owned by Charlotte Booth. Not only does Charlotte make great jams and jellies, but she bakes up a storm, too. I first sampled this delicious bar cookie when I dropped in to buy a jar of apricot jam. I went home with the apricot and a jar of cherry preserves—as well as this recipe.

INGREDIENTS
1 ½ cups all-purpose flour
¼ cup firmly packed (dark or light) brown sugar
⅛ teaspoon salt
6 tablespoons vegetable oil
2 tablespoons water
½ teaspoon almond extract
¾ cup cherry preserves
cooking spray

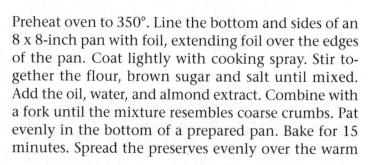

TOPPING
½ cup chopped almonds
¼ cup brown sugar
2 tablespoons vegetable oil

Preheat oven to 350°. Line the bottom and sides of an 8 x 8-inch pan with foil, extending foil over the edges of the pan. Coat lightly with cooking spray. Stir together the flour, brown sugar and salt until mixed. Add the oil, water, and almond extract. Combine with a fork until the mixture resembles coarse crumbs. Pat evenly in the bottom of a prepared pan. Bake for 15 minutes. Spread the preserves evenly over the warm crust. Mix the almonds, brown sugar, and oil until the mixture resembles coarse crumbs. Sprinkle over the top of the preserves. Bake for another 20 minutes. Cool completely. Lift out of pan using the foil. Store wrapped in the refrigerator.

Yield: 16 bars.

CIDER CAKE

I admit it, when my aunt Lizzie told me she was going to bake a cake and deliberately add cider, I was skeptical, but I'm happy to say how wrong my first impression was. I hope you'll feel the same when you try this lovely cake.

INGREDIENTS
½ cup butter
½ cup granulated sugar
2 eggs
1 cup self-rising flour
1 teaspoon baking soda
½ - ¾ teaspoon of spice (your favorite: nutmeg, cinnamon, ginger, or allspice)*
¾ cup apple cider

Preheat oven to 350°. Sift the flour, soda and spice and set aside. Cream together the butter and sugar, add the eggs one at a time and beat until light and fluffy. Fold in half of the dry sifted ingredients, stir in the cider, and then fold in the remaining flour mixture. Pour into two 8 inch cake pans that have been lined with parchment paper. Bake for 20 minutes or until a toothpick comes out clean. Serve warm or cold with whipped cream. (*The cake varies in taste depending on what kind of cider and/or amount of spice used.)
Yield: 6-8 servings.

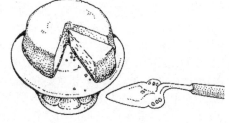

COCONUT CARROT CAKE

I first made this cake for my late husband Chad. It was to be a lonely first Thanksgiving for us together. His mother had gone on a cruise with friends, and my aunt had died just the year before. I felt sad and lonely and turned to my oven for comfort. I found it in this decadent recipe. Despite the fact it was just the two of us, we ate that cake for breakfast, and as dessert for both lunch and dinner that whole holiday weekend. The pumpkin pie was forgotten and making this cake became a holiday tradition.

INGREDIENTS

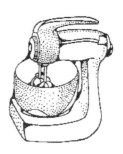

2 cups flour
2 ½ teaspoon baking soda
2 teaspoon cinnamon
1 teaspoon salt
1 cup oil*
2 cups sugar
3 eggs
1 can (8 ounces) crushed pineapple in juice—
     drained
2 cups grated carrots
1 ⅓ cup sweetened coconut
½ cup chopped walnuts
cooking spray

Spray a bundt pan with cooking spray. Preheat oven to 350°. Mix flour, baking soda, cinnamon and salt together in a large bowl. In a separate bowl, beat oil, sugar and eggs at medium speed until thoroughly blended. Add flour mixture and beat until smooth. Add pineapple, carrots, coconut, and nuts. Pour into bundt pan and bake 50-60 minutes or until tester comes out clean. Cool for 10 minutes. Remove from

pan and completely cool on rack before frosting. However, this cake is so rich, it really doesn't need any other adornment. Sift a little confectioners' sugar over it if desired. (*This will never be a diet dessert, but you can exchange the oil for unsweetened applesauce. The cake will taste just as good but will be a bit more moist.)
Yield: 10-12 servings.

MAPLE FROSTING (optional)

INGREDIENTS
2 tablespoons butter, softened
2 tablespoons maple or pancake syrup (pure maple
    syrup is best!)
1 ½ cups confectioners' sugar

Beat butter and syrup in medium bowl until blended. Gradually beat in conectioners' sugar until smooth.
Yield: 1 ½ cups

COCONUT GRAHAM BARS

Did I mention I'm absolutely nuts about coconut? That's why I make so many different recipes using this wonderful sweet fruit of the coconut. (Can you say that about a nut?) Anyway, these are wonderful. You won't be able to eat just one.

INGREDIENTS
2 cups graham cracker crumbs
½ cup granulated sugar
½ cup butter, melted
2 cups flaked coconut
1 can (14 ounces) sweetened condensed milk

TOPPING
1 ½ cups brown sugar, packed
6 tablespoons heavy whipping cream
¼ cup butter, cubed
¾ cup milk chocolate chips

Preheat oven to 350°. In a small bowl, combine the graham cracker crumbs, sugar, and butter. Press into the bottom of a greased 13 x 9 x 2 inch baking pan for 8-10 minutes or until lightly browned. Combine the coconut and milk; spread over the warm crust. Bake for 12-15 minutes or until the edges are lightly browned. Cool on a wire rack. Meanwhile, in a large saucepan, combine the brown sugar, cream and butter. Bring to a boil over medium heat, stirring constantly. Boil for 1 minute. Remove the mixture from the heat. Stir in the chocolate chips until melted. Spread over the coconut layer. Cool before cutting. Yield: 4 ½ dozen bars.

COCONUT MACAROONS

Are you sensing a theme with these last few recipes? Yes, I'm a certifiable coconut … nut! And these coconut macaroons are not only easy to make, they're wonderful. They're great for dessert, afternoon tea, or—just snacking. They look great on a holiday cookie plate, too.

INGREDIENTS
3 egg whites
¼ teaspoon cream of tartar
⅛ teaspoon salt
¾ cup granulated sugar
¼ almond extract
2 cups flaked coconut
12 candied cherries, cut into quarters

Preheat oven to 300°. Grease cookie sheet lightly. Beat the egg whites, cream of tartar, and salt in a medium bowl until foamy. Beat in the sugar, 1 tablespoon at a time. Continue beating until stiff and glossy. Do not underbeat. Fold in the almond extract and coconut. Drop mixture by teaspoonfuls about 1 inch apart onto a foil-lined baking sheet. Place a cherry piece on each cookie. Bake for 20-25 minutes or just until edges are light brown. Cool for 10 minutes; remove from the baking sheets.
Yield: 3 ½ to 4 dozen cookies.

AMBROSIA PUDDING

When Vance Ingram's wife Janie heard I was putting this cookbook together, she could hardly contain her enthusiasm. "Katie, ya gotta put in my memaw's Ambrosia pudding recipe. Ya just gotta!" she pleaded. So . . . here it is.

INGREDIENTS
2 cups cold milk
1 package (1.5 ounces) instant vanilla pudding mix
¼ cup honey
2 teaspoons grated orange peel
¼ teaspoon vanilla extract
1 cup whipping cream, whipped
1 medium firm banana, sliced
1 can (11 ounces) mandarin orange sections, drained
¼ cup flaked coconut
¼ cup sliced almonds
¼ cup mini marshmallows

In a bowl, blend milk and pudding mix according to the package instructions. Add the honey, orange peel, and vanilla extract. Fold in the whipped cream and marshmallows. In individual dessert dishes (parfait glasses look really pretty), layer half of the pudding, banana slices, orange sections, coconut, and almonds. Repeat the layers. Chill.
Yield: 4-6 servings.

MOLASSES COOKIES

I have to admit, I love old-fashioned cookies, pies, and old recipe books. Molasses cookies always remind me of days gone by. Maybe I saw someone eat them in a movie. Yes, a little girl in a feed-sack dress and dark braids. The movie was in black and white, so you know it was old, and to her molasses cookies were the ultimate comfort food. I love the way they crack when baking, and how pretty the sugar looks. And there's no better treat than to dunk them in a tall glass of ice-cold milk. This recipe has never failed me.

INGREDIENTS
¾ cup shortening
1 ¼ cup sugar, divided
1 egg
¼ cup molasses
2 tablespoons milk
1 teaspoon vanilla extract
2 ½ cups all-purpose flour
1 ½ teaspoons baking soda
1 teaspoon ground cinnamon
¾ teaspoon salt
¾ teaspoon ground nutmeg

In a large mixing bowl, cream shortening and 1 cup sugar. Beat in the egg, molasses, milk and vanilla. Combine the flour, baking soda, cinnamon, salt and nutmeg; gradually add to creamed mixture. Cover and refrigerate for 1 hour. Roll into 1 ¼ inch balls; roll in remaining sugar. Place 2 inches apart on greased baking sheets. Bake at 350° for 10-14 minutes or until tops crack and edges are slightly firm. Remove to wire racks to cool.
Yield: 5 dozen cookies.

FINGER-LICKING FINE COFFEE CAKE

Nona Fiske was sweet on the former manager of Artisans Alley, the late Ezra Hilton. She would get up early to bake him his favorite coffee cake and walk it across the Square. Of course, their friendship rather soured when Ezra took up with Mary Elliott, the owner of Tea and Tasties, the Square's tea shop. Still, Nona has brought this lovely cake to a couple of the Square's potluck dinners and it truly is finger-licking fine.

INGREDIENTS
2 ¼ cups all-purpose flour
1 ½ cups granulated sugar (divided)
2 teaspoons baking powder
½ teaspoon baking soda
¼ teaspoon salt
1 teaspoon ground cinnamon
5 tablespoons butter, softened
⅓ cup vegetable oil (or you can substitute the same
    amount of unsweetened applesauce)
2 large eggs
1 cup light sour cream
2 teaspoons vanilla extract
½ cup chopped walnuts (optional)

Preheat oven to 350°. Grease a 9 or 10 inch tube or bundt pan (also works well in a 9 x 13 inch rectangular pan).

In a small bowl combine the walnuts, cinnamon, and half a cup of sugar. Set aside. In a medium-sized bowl, combine the flour, baking powder, baking soda, and salt. Set aside.

In a large mixing bowl, beat the butter, oil (or applesauce) and the remaining 1 cup of sugar until well mixed. Add the eggs one at a time, beating well after each addition. Reduce mixer speed to low and gradually beat in the flour mixture, the sour cream, and the vanilla, but do not over beat the mixture.

Spoon half the batter into prepared baking pan. Sprinkle with half the nut and cinnamon mixture. Spoon the remaining batter into the pan and sprinkle with the rest of the nut mixture.

Bake the cake for 55-65 minutes, or until a toothpick comes out clean. (35-40 minutes if using the 9 x 13 inch pan.) Cut in wedges and serve warm.
Yield: 10-12 servings.

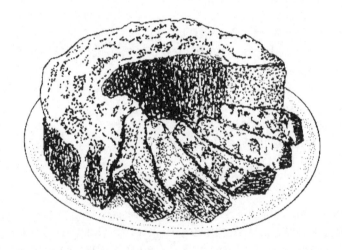

OATMEAL RAISIN NUT COOKIES

As a Scot, my aunt Lizzie believed in adding oatmeal to almost everything she baked—with mixed results. But she liked to experiment and she figured if you put enough butter on it, it would taste good anyway. There's no doubt that these cookies won't last long in your cookie jar.

INGREDIENTS
¾ cup butter, softened
¾ cup sugar
¾ cup packed light brown sugar
2 eggs
1 teaspoon vanilla extract
1 ¼ cups all-purpose flour
1 teaspoon baking soda
¾ teaspoon ground cinnamon
¼ teaspoon allspice
½ teaspoon salt
2 ¾ cups rolled or quick oats
1 cup raisins
1 cup chopped walnuts

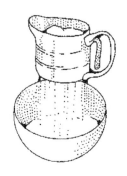

Preheat oven to 375°. In large bowl, cream together the butter and sugars until smooth. Beat in the eggs and vanilla until fluffy. Stir together the flour, baking soda, cinnamon, allspice, and salt. Gradually beat into the butter mixture. Stir in oats, raisins, and walnuts. Drop by teaspoonfuls onto ungreased cookie sheets. Bake 10-12 minutes or until golden brown. Cool slightly, and then remove from sheet to wire rack. Cool completely.
Yield: 4 dozen cookies.

PUMPKIN CHIFFON PIE

Let's face it, by the time you've made it through the appetizers, the turkey, stuffing, mashed potatoes and gravy, who has room for Thanksgiving dessert? With this light and creamy pumpkin pie, you will.

INGREDIENTS
2 ¾ cups cold milk
2 packages (1.5 ounces each) instant vanilla pudding
1 can (15 ounces) pumpkin
1 teaspoon ground cinnamon
½ teaspoon ground ginger
¼ teaspoon ground cloves
1 prepared graham cracker crust (9 inches)
frozen whipped topping (thawed) optional
additional cinnamon for dusting (optional)

In a large mixing bowl, combine the milk and pudding mixes. Beat for 1 minute (the mixture will thicken). Add the pumpkin and spices; beat 1 minute longer. Pour into the piecrust. Cover and refrigerate for 2 hours or until firm. If desired, garnish with whipped topping and sprinkle with cinnamon.
Yield: 6-8 servings.

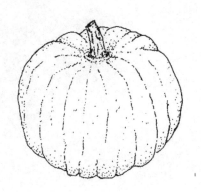

PEANUT BUTTER BUCKEYES

I get jittery if I can't bake and in the summer sometimes it's just too hot to crank up the oven. That's when I make these delicious and incredibly easy peanut butter buckeyes. When I bring them into Artisans Alley, they seem to disappear in only minutes.

INGREDIENTS
1 (18 ounce) jar creamy peanut butter
½ cup butter (softened)
1 pound of confectioners' sugar
1 tablespoon vanilla
12 ounces semi-sweet chocolate chips
2 tablespoons vegetable shortening

Cream the peanut butter and butter. Add the sugar and vanilla and mix well. Form into 1 inch balls and refrigerate. Melt the chocolate chips and shortening in a double boiler or in the microwave. Dip the peanut butter balls into chocolate with a toothpick about ¾ of the way covered. Place chocolate side down on waxed paper. Let them set at room temperature or refrigerate.
Yield: About 5 dozen pieces.

RASPBERRY SUPREME

Another hot-weather recipe that'll cool you right off is Raspberry Supreme. It couldn't be easier to make, and your guests will think you fussed. Best of all, there aren't a lot of calories, either. (Well, if you top it with whipped cream, all bets are off.)

INGREDIENTS
1 package (3 ounces) raspberry gelatin
½ cup boiling water
1 cup crushed ice, drained of excess water
fresh or frozen raspberries
fresh mint leaves (optional)

Chill dessert dishes or sherbet glasses in the refrigerator. Put the gelatin in the blender; add boiling water. Cover the blender and blend until the gelatin is dissolved. Keep the blender running and slowly add the crushed ice. Blend for about 1 minute, or until the container feels cool to the  touch. Place several fresh raspberries in the chilled dessert dishes or sherbet glasses, pour the raspberry fluff mixture over the raspberries and then garnish with a few fresh raspberries. If desired, garnish with a sprig of fresh mint.
Yield: 4 servings.

RUTH'S PEANUT BUTTER COOKIES

My aunt Lizzie's best friend was Ruth Mathews, who lived next door to us. Ruth was like a part of the family and loved to bake as much as my aunt and me. If she borrowed a cup of sugar, she never returned it without a plate of cookies or half a cake.

Nobody made peanut butter cookies like Ruth, and I was thrilled when, as a ten-year old, she shared this recipe with me.

INGREDIENTS
1 cup shortening
1 cup peanut butter
1 cup sugar
1 cup brown sugar
2 eggs
2 ½ cups all-purpose flour
1 teaspoons baking powder
1 ½ teaspoon baking soda
½ teaspoon salt

Preheat oven to 375°. In a large bowl, combine shortening, peanut butter, sugars, and eggs. Mix well. In another bowl, sift together the flour, baking powder, baking soda, and salt. Slowly stir into the sugar butter mixture until a dough forms. Chill the dough for at least an hour. Shape the dough into 1 ¼ inch balls. Place about 3 inches apart on foil or parchment lined cookie sheet. Flatten in a crisscross pattern with the back of a fork. Bake until light brown, 9-10 minutes. (For chewier cookies, bake at 300°F for 15 minutes.) Cool on baking sheets for a minute; transfer to a rack to cool completely.
Yield: About 3 dozen.

PECAN OATMEAL PIE

Jordan Tanner owns Tanner's—the bakery right on Victoria Square. Every day wonderful aromas fill the Square. One of his specialties during the holidays is pecan oatmeal pie. I managed to cajole the recipe out of him and it tastes just as good as the ones that come straight from his bakery's ovens. Maybe it'll become a favorite at your holiday table as well.

INGREDIENTS

2 eggs
½ cup granulated sugar
½ cup brown sugar, packed
¾ cup light corn syrup
½ cup milk
¼ cup butter, melted
1 teaspoon vanilla extract
pinch of salt
2 cups pecan halves
¾ cup quick-cooking oats
½ cup flaked coconut
1 unbaked 9-inch pastry shell

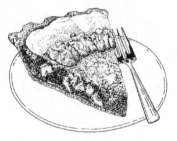

Preheat the oven to 350°. In a large bowl, whisk the eggs and sugars. Gradually whisk in the corn syrup, milk, butter, vanilla, and salt. Stir in the pecans, oats, and coconut. Pour into the pastry shell. Bake for 45-50 minutes or until a knife inserted near the center comes out clean. (Cover the edges of the crust with aluminum foil if necessary to prevent overbrowning.) Cool on a wire rack.
Yield: 8 servings.

PEPPERMINT PATTIES

If you love to make your own candy, this is a wonderful, easy recipe, and they taste even better than the commercial version. I made these for the vendors at Artisans Alley several times during the holidays and they disappeared within minutes. I'm pretty sure you'll have the same results when you serve them to your family and friends.

INGREDIENTS
3 ¾ cups confectioners' sugar
3 tablespoons butter, softened
2 to 3 teaspoons peppermint extract
½ teaspoon vanilla extract
¼ cup evaporated milk
2 cups (12 ounces) semisweet chocolate chips
2 tablespoons shortening

In a large bowl, combine the first four ingredients. Add the evaporated milk and mix well. Roll into 1-inch balls and place on a waxed paper-lined baking sheet. Flatten balls with a glass to ¼ inch. Cover and freeze for 30 minutes. In a heavy saucepan or microwave, melt chocolate chips and shortening on low heat; stir until smooth. Dip the patties, allowing the excess to drip off. Place the patties on the waxed paper. Let them stand until set.
Yield: 5 dozen patties.

RHUBARB CRISP

My aunt Lizzie always had a large stand of rhubarb growing out in the yard. How we looked forward to spring and that first batch of rhubarb crisp. She also made rhubarb crumble, rhubarb bread, and rhubarb chutney, but it was the crisp that I liked best. Here's her recipe.

INGREDIENTS:
1 cup light brown sugar, firmly packed
1 cup all-purpose flour
¾ cup quick cooking rolled oats
½ cup melted butter
1 teaspoon cinnamon
4 cups sliced rhubarb
1 cup granulated sugar
2 tablespoons cornstarch
1 cup water
1 teaspoon vanilla

Preheat oven to 350°. In mixing bowl, combine the brown sugar, flour, oats, butter, and cinnamon; mix together until crumbly. Press half of the brown sugar and oats mixture into a buttered 8-inch square baking dish. Top with the sliced rhubarb. In a saucepan combine 1 cup granulated sugar, cornstarch, and the 1 cup of water and vanilla. Cook together until the liquid is clear, then pour over the rhubarb. Top the rhubarb with remaining crumb mixture and bake for 45 to 55 minutes. Serve warm, and if desired, with a scoop of ice cream or a dollop of whipped cream.
Yield: 4-6 servings.

STRAWBERRY SHORTCAKE

Is there a more photogenic fruit other than the strawberry? (Okay, watermelon comes close.) And there's nothing like fresh-picked, locally grown strawberries, which we have in abundance right here in McKinlay Mill. This recipe is easy to make, too.

INGREDIENTS
3-4 cups sugared sliced strawberries
1 cup whipping cream, whipped (or commercial
    whipped topping)

SHORTCAKE INGREDIENTS
2 cups sifted all-purpose flour
2 tablespoons sugar
3 teaspoons baking powder
½ teaspoon salt
½ cup butter
1 egg
⅔ cup milk

Preheat oven to 450°. Sift together the flour, sugar, baking power, and salt. Cut in the butter until the mixture resembles course crumbs. Beat egg and milk together; add to dry mixture; stir just enough to moisten. Spread the dough in a greased 8 inch round pan, building up the edges slightly. Bake for 15-18 minutes. Remove from the pan; cook on rack for 5 minutes. Split in two layers. Lift the top off carefully. Butter the bottom layer. Spoon the berries and cream between layers and over the top. Serve while the shortcake is still warm.
Yield: 6-8 servings.

APPLE CRISP

One of the best things about autumn is the bounty of the harvest. All the fruits and vegetables I like best are available fresh at the local farmer's market which comes to Victoria Square.

I love the smell of baking apples—especially when you add cinnamon to the mix. Don't like apples? Try substituting fresh peaches. (Unlike the previous crisp recipe, this one doesn't need the simple syrup to counteract the fruit's tartness.)

INGREDIENTS
4 cups sliced pared tart apples (about 4 medium)
⅔ to ¾ cup brown sugar, firmly packed
½ cup all-purpose flour
½ cup quick oats
¾ teaspoon cinnamon
¾ teaspoon nutmeg
⅓ cup butter, softened

Preheat the oven to 375°. Grease an 8 x 8 x 2-inch baking pan. Place the apple slices in the pan. Mix the remaining ingredients thoroughly. It will resemble coarse crumbs. Sprinkle the mixture over the apples. Bake for 30 minutes or until the apples are tender and the topping is golden brown. Serve warm, and if desired, with a scoop of ice cream, a dollop of whipped cream, or pour on a little light cream. It's a simple but decadent dessert.

Yield: 4-6 servings.

CUT-OUT COOKIES

What holiday would be complete without cut-out cookies—and I mean all of them. Thanksgiving, Christmas, Valentine's Day, St. Patrick's Day, Easter, Flag Day, 4th of July, and birthdays—don't forget birthdays! You can't eat a cut-out cookie and not smile. I've made this recipe since I was ten or eleven, and I've amassed quite a collection of cookie cutters over the years. Copper, aluminum, plastic—most of which were bought at yard sales. They all work and the cookies are met with grins of pleasure.

INGREDIENTS
1 ⅓ cups of granulated sugar
1 teaspoon of vanilla or almond extract*
1 ⅓ cups of shortening
4 slightly beaten eggs
4 cups of all-purpose flour
1 teaspoon of salt
3 teaspoons of baking powder

Mix all the ingredients together until it forms a ball. Place the dough in a plastic bag or covered bowl. Refrigerate for four hours or overnight.

Preheat the oven to 350°. On a floured board, roll out the dough to about ¼ inch thickness. Cut out shapes with cookie cutters of your choice. Bake for 8-10 minutes or until the edges just start to brown. Cool on wire racks. When completely cooled, frost. If you wish to add colored sugars, do so before you bake the dough. (*Feel free to substitute any flavored extract—they all work equally well.)
Yield varies depending on the size of the cookies.

FRENCH CRUMB CAKE

Every Christmas morning, my aunt Lizzie would bake a pan of French crumb cake. It just wouldn't be Christmas morning without it. Of course, with such a big recipe, we had crumb cake to spare—and shared it with our neighbors, but still there was more than we could eat. Luckily, this recipe freezes well—because a month later we were grateful to have a piece for breakfast and feel the holiday spirit all over again.

INGREDIENTS
2 tablespoons vegetable oil
4 cups all-purpose flour (divided)
½ cup granulated sugar
2 ½ teaspoons baking powder
½ teaspoon salt
1 large egg
½ cup milk
2 teaspoons vanilla extract
1 cup light brown sugar, firmly packed
1 ½ teaspoons ground cinnamon
1 cup butter, melted and cooled
confectioners' sugar for dusting
cooking spray

Place the rack in the center of your oven and preheat oven to 325°. Spray a 9 x 13 x 2-inch baking pan with cooking spray, dust with flour, and tap out the excess. Set aside. In a medium bowl, sift together 1 ½ cups flour, the granulated sugar, baking powder, and salt, and set aside. In a bowl, whisk together the egg, milk, vegetable oil, and vanilla. Fold the dry ingredients into the egg mixture. Spread the batter evenly into the prepared pan and set aside. Pour melted butter over the remaining flour mixture and mix until large crumbs form. Sprinkle the crumbs over the batter and bake, rotating the pan after 10 minutes. Continue baking until a toothpick comes out clean (about 10 minutes or more). Transfer the pan to a wire rack to cool. Dust with confectioners' sugar. Cut into 3-inch squares using a serrated knife. Serve. Store any leftovers in an airtight container for up to 3 days.
Yield: 24 pieces.

BOURBON BALLS

This recipe came from our neighbor Ruth. She was famous for serving these at Christmastime, although I
think she may have upped the amount of bourbon
she added to the recipe. (You could tell how many she
ate by the loudness of her cackle, too.) You can substitute blended whiskey or even rum for the bourbon
and they taste just as good.

INGREDIENTS
1 cup walnuts
2 ¼ cups vanilla wafer cookies,
    crumbled
1 cup confectioners' sugar
1 tablespoon cocoa powder
1 tablespoon white corn syrup
¾ cup bourbon
¼ cup additional confectioners' sugar

Mix together the first four ingredients then add the
corn syrup and bourbon and blend thoroughly. (It
will form a dough) Let stand for 45 minutes. Roll into
1-inch balls. Roll the balls in the ¼ cup of confectioners' sugar. Refrigerate for 4-5 days. Before serving,
roll the bourbon balls in confectioners' sugar once
again.
Yield: 4 dozen.

VICTORIAN SPONGE CAKE

I once visited a tea room in Ontario, Canada that served a version of this lovely cake. I was determined to figure out a similar recipe and this is what I came up with. It's delightful.

INGREDIENTS
2 cups cake flour
2 teaspoons baking powder
¼ teaspoon salt
zest from ½ lemon
1 cup unsalted butter, softened
4 eggs (room temperature)
2 tablespoons warm milk
¼ teaspoon vanilla

FILLING
1 cup strawberry (or your favorite) jam
1 cup heavy cream, whipped
confectioners' sugar for garnish
fruit for garnish (optional)

The sponge cake: Preheat oven to 350°. Lightly butter and flour two 8 x 1 inch round layer cake pans. Sift the flour, baking power, and salt together twice. In a food processor, process lemon zest and granulated sugar until finely ground (about one minute). Pour into large mixing bowl. Using an electric mixer, beat at medium speed until light and fluffy (about 3 minutes). Set aside.

In 2-cup measuring cup, whisk the eggs, milk and vanilla. Add to the butter mixture, 2 tablespoons at a time, beating well after each addition and adding 1 tablespoon flour mixture during the last three additions. Gradually beat in remaining flour mixture, beating until smooth and shiny. Pour into pans and smooth tops. Bake for 25-30 minutes until top is golden brown and springs back when lightly touched in the center. Cool in pans on racks for 10 minutes. Remove the cake from the pans and cool on wire racks.

To ASSEMBLE THE CAKE:
Invert 1 cooled cake layer on a serving plate. Spread with jam, then whipped cream, leaving a 1-inch border around the edge of the cake. Top with the second cake layer, right side up. Place an 8-inch lacy paper doily on top of cake. Sift confectioners' sugar over the top of the cake. Carefully lift the doily. Or, if desired, ice top of cake with whipped cream. If desired, garnish with fruit to match your jam.
Yield: 6-8 servings.

SNACKS

CARAMEL CORN

One of the things I loved to eat when I was growing up was caramel corn. My ever-frugal aunt Lizzie would never consider buying the packaged stuff. "You don't know what's in it," she'd say, and proceed to make a batch every couple of months. And you know, it tastes better when it's homemade. I hope you'll try this version that I've come to love.

INGREDIENTS
8 cups popped corn (about ½ cup unpopped)
¾ cup granulated sugar
¾ cup brown sugar (packed)
½ cup light corn syrup
½ cup water
1 teaspoon white vinegar
¼ teaspoon salt
¾ cup butter

Measure popped corn into a large baking sheet. Combine the sugars, corn syrup, water, vinegar, and salt in a 2-quart saucepan. Heat to boiling over medium high heat, stirring frequently. Cook, stirring constantly until your candy thermometer reaches 260° (or until a small amount of mixture dropped into very cold water forms a hard ball). Reduce the heat to low; stir in the butter until melted. Pour the syrup over the popped corn. Stir until it's well coated. Spread the mixture on the baking sheet and allow to cool. Break into pieces. Store in an airtight container. (Make about 1 ¾ pounds.) For a nutty variation, sprinkle 1 and ½ cups of your favorite nuts over the popcorn before you pour the syrup mixture. (We liked to use unsalted mixed nuts or 1 ½ cups of peanuts. Yum-Yum!) Yield: 8 cups.

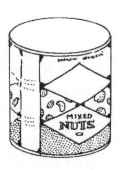

CARAMEL APPLES

The south shore of Lake Ontario is famous for being a fruit belt. Apples, peaches, cherries, grapes—we've got it all. A great autumn treat is caramel apples, and they couldn't be easier to make. Kids love them—and adults like them, too.

INGREDIENTS

4 or 5 medium apples
1 package (14 ounces) caramel candies
½ teaspoon salt
2 tablespoons of water
wooden skewers or popsicle sticks

Wash and thoroughly dry the apples. Remove the stem and blossom end on each of them. In the top half of a double boiler (bottom filled with water, of course), heat the caramels, salt, and water, stirring frequently until the caramels are melted and the mixture is smooth. Insert the skewers ¾ of the way through the apples (blossom side). With the sauce still over the hot water, dip each apple into the hot caramel sauce. Spoon sauce over the top until it is completely covered. Remove from sauce and place on waxed paper. Chill the apples until the coating is firm. (Best if eaten a day or two after making.)

Yield: 4-5 servings.

CHOCOLATE DIP

Who doesn't love chocolate? And who doesn't love fruit dipped in chocolate? This is a great summer treat and always looks elegant.

INGREDIENTS
1 package (8 ounces) cream cheese, softened
⅓ cup granulated sugar
⅓ cup baking cocoa
1 teaspoon vanilla extract
2 cups whipped topping
assorted fruit for dipping

In a large bowl, beat the cream cheese and sugar until it is smooth. Beat in the cocoa and vanilla. Fold in the whipped topping until the mixture is smooth. Serve with fruit (such as fresh bananas, strawberries, cherries, etc.)
Yield: 2 cups

CURRY DIP

I love curry. No lie! But don't worry, curry doesn't always have to mean a dish is "hot," just fragrant and delicious. I'm always looking for new ways to incorporate this versatile spice into my favorite foods. This was a no-brainer for me. I've made it for parties, for watching football games, and just to snack on while I'm baking. (Keeps one from licking the beaters.) I hope you enjoy it as much as I do.

INGREDIENTS
1 carton plain yogurt
½ cup mayonnaise
1 ½ - 2 teaspoons curry powder
¼ teaspoon chili powder
¼ teaspoon ground ginger
¼ teaspoon turmeric
⅛ teaspoon salt

Combine all ingredients. Mix well. Cover and refrigerate for at least one hour. Serve dip with cut fresh vegetables.
Yield: 1 ½ cups.

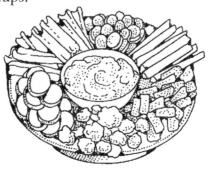

FOUR CHEESE BEER SPREAD

When you own and operate a pizza parlor, like Andy Rust does, you work three hundred and sixty four days of the year. You work during every sports season. You work on your birthday. You work every day but Christmas. So, guess what Andy makes every Christmas?

INGREDIENTS
2 cups (8 ounces) shredded sharp cheddar cheese
2 cups (8 ounces) shredded process American cheese
1 (3 ounce) package cream cheese, softened
¼ (4 ounce) package blue cheese, crumbled
¾ cup beer
2 tablespoons minced onions
1 large clove garlic, crushed
1 teaspoon hot sauce

Combine all ingredients. Mix well. Cover and refrigerate for at least one hour. Serve with crackers.
Yield: 1 ¾ cups.

ROASTED CHICKPEAS

Of all the beans out there, I'm partial to chickpeas. This recipe is so incredibly easy to make, and the results so fine, that I make them quite often—and I don't always share.

INGREDIENTS
2 cups cooked garbanzo beans (drained and rinsed if canned)
¼ teaspoon garlic powder
⅛ teaspoon pepper flakes
cooking spray

Preheat oven to 350°. Light coat a lined baking sheet with cooking spray. Spread the chickpeas on the tray and sprinkle with the garlic powder and pepper flakes. Toss to coat. Roast on the bottom rack of the oven for 45-50 minutes, turning the chickpeas about every 15 minutes until brown and crunchy. Cool before serving. Store for up to a week in an airtight container. Yield: 2 cups.

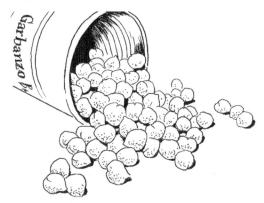

SWEET SUE'S TOFFEE SQUARES

When I've got a hankering for sweets (and boy do I ever), I often visit Sweet Sue's Confectionary on Victoria Square. Sometimes the aroma of chocolate almost lifts me off my feet, it's that enticing. There's a reason Sue gained her nick-name—she's terribly sweet, just like her candies. And it was sweet of her to share this easy recipe that I've often made myself.

INGREDIENTS
1 cup butter (softened)
1 cup packed brown sugar (dark or light)
1 egg yolk
1 teaspoon vanilla extract
2 cups all-purpose flour
¼ teaspoon salt
8 ounces of semi-sweet chocolate chips
½ cup chopped nuts

Preheat oven to 350°. In a mixing bowl, cream the butter and sugar. Add the egg yolk, vanilla, flour, and salt and mix well. Spread into a greased 9 x 13 x 2-inch baking pan. Bake for 20-25 minutes or until golden brown. Melt the chocolate in a heavy saucepan over very low heat stirring constantly. (You can also melt the chocolate in the microwave.) Spread the chocolate over the hot bars. Immediately sprinkle with the nuts. Cool. Cut into 1 inch squares.
Yield: About 9 dozen pieces.

SPICY POPCORN SNACK MIX

Liz Meier is Artisans Alley's resident stained glass artist. She makes beautiful sun catchers, ornaments, and stained glass panels with vibrant gardens and wildlife. She also repairs vintage stained glass. When she's not in her workshop, she relaxes in front of the tube watching old movies with her husband and son. She tells me this is their favorite snack.

INGREDIENTS
2 ½ quarts popped popcorn (about 1 ¼ cups un-
    popped popcorn), divided
2 cups corn chips
1 cup dry roasted peanuts
¼ cup butter, cubed
2 tablespoons hot sauce
1 teaspoon celery seed

Preheat oven to 350°. In a large bowl, combine 2 cups popcorn, corn chips and peanuts. In a small saucepan, melt the butter; add the hot sauce and celery seed. Remove from the heat. Pour over the popcorn mixture and toss to coat. Transfer the mixture to a greased 15x 10 x 1-inch baking pan. Bake for 10-15 minutes or until crisp. Place in a large bowl. Add the remaining popcorn and toss to coat. Store in an airtight container.
Yield: 2 ½ quarts

SHRIMP SPREAD

Edie Silver brought this cracker spread to Artisans Alley at holiday time. It looks so festive with the green onions, red tomatoes, and tiny shrimp. It's easy to make and tastes great.

INGREDIENTS
1 package (8 ounces) cream cheese
½ cup sour cream
¼ cup mayonnaise
1 cup seafood cocktail sauce
2 cups shredded mozzarella cheese
2 cans (4 ¼ ounces each) shrimp, rinsed and drained
3 green onions, chopped
¾ cup finely chopped tomato

In a small mixing bowl, beat the cream cheese, sour cream and mayonnaise until smooth. Spread on a large (12-inch) serving platter. Cover with seafood sauce. Sprinkle on the cheese, shrimp, onions, and tomato. Cover and chill for at least two hours. Serve with crackers.
Yield: 8 servings.

SPICY SNACK MIX

Now I don't mean to come off like the Food Police, but let's face it, too much of our processed food is high in sodium. That's one of the beautiful things about making our own food—we can control the amount of salt we take in. This recipe does contain seasoned salt, but I've cut it in half and it still tastes great. Also, you can vary the other ingredients to give it more bite if you like. It travels well and is great for parties.

INGREDIENTS
½ cup butter
1 ½ teaspoon seasoned salt
1 tablespoon Worcestershire sauce
½ to 1 teaspoon garlic powder
½ to 1 teaspoon hot pepper sauce
6 cups Rice Chex cereal
5 cups Cheerios cereal
5 cups Wheat Chex cereal
2 cups mini pretzel sticks or bagel chips
1 12-ounce can of lightly salted mixed nuts

Preheat oven to 250°. In a small saucepan, melt the butter. Add seasoned salt, Worcestershire sauce, garlic powder and hot pepper sauce. Set aside. In a large mixing bowl, combine the cereals and nuts. Mix well. Stir in the butter mixture until well blended. Spread into two large baking pans. Bake for one hour, stirring the mixture every 15 minutes.
Yield: 20 cups.

TEA TIME

A NICE CUP OF TEA

In order to have tea time you must have tea. Believe it or not, there's a proper way to make a pot of tea.

I must admit, I'm not really educated when it comes to the various teas of the world. In my aunt's home, we always drank English tea (either Typhoo or PG Tips). To me, herbal teas taste like what they are: dried weeds and leaves. Yes, I know that a cup of orange pekoe is also a brew of steeped leaves, but for me it's a magical drink. I drink it to celebrate. I drink it to console. I drink it for comfort. I drink it on a  daily basis. Start the day without my cup of tea? That's blasphemy! I prefer black teas (see above), and I've read where they contain the most caffeine, although far less than your average cup of coffee. So if you're avoiding caffeine, stick with green or white teas.

In order to have a good cup of tea you need a couple of basic ingredients: tea, water, and a teapot. (It doesn't hurt to have a good tea kettle, either. Electric works best as it's the fastest way to boil water.)

And what are the steps for making a good pot of tea?

Fill your tea kettle with enough water to fill your tea pot. Boil the water. It must be boiled otherwise the tea won't steep properly. When the water gets pretty hot but not yet boiling, pour some into your waiting teapot. (Or as my aunt used to say, "you must scald the teapot.") When the water in your kettle is about to boil, discard the warm water in the teapot. Place one teabag (or more if it's a large pot) into the teapot. When the water boils—don't wait!—pour the water onto the tea. You don't need more teabags (or loose tea) to make a stronger cup. It's the length of time the tea brews that makes it stronger.

When the tea is the strength you prefer, pour it into your cup. You can doctor it anyway you like with milk, cream, lemon, sugar, or honey. Stir. Sit back and enjoy your nice cuppa. And while you're drinking your tea you can rejoice in the knowledge that a number of studies have shown that tea is good for you, too!

TEACUP OR MUG?

I think there's nothing lovelier than setting the table with beautiful bone china. Don't tell Andy, but I have quite a collection of teacups, sugar and creamer sets, and mismatched china plates. Some of them belonged to my great aunt, but many of them I picked up at antique stores, estate, and yard sales. Of course, the nicest ones are made in Eng-land—at least in my not-so-humble opinion. And I will admit that when I look at my accumulated collection, I see that I tend to collect cups with lovely roses on them. And, of course, since my goal was to one day open a bed and breakfast (the English Ivy Inn) and offer an afternoon tea, I have more than a couple with an ivy motif.

But let's face it, when you're in a hurry, who has time to hand wash that lovely cup and saucer before leaving for work? And I couldn't very well take a bone china cup to my day job. I have a number of service-able mugs, usually a souvenir from somewhere I've traveled. (Hey, I even have one from the *Haven't Got a Clue* mystery bookshop in Stoneham, New Hampshire!)

Of course just about everything goes better with a cup of tea, and following are a few of my favorite tea-time recipes.

AUNT LIZZIE'S CREAM SCONES

My aunt Lizzie only made these scones for special occasions. Birthday breakfasts, for Christmas tea—I never understood why, because I liked her scones with fruit or nuts better. But for her, cream scones were SPECIAL and there was no arguing with her. Okay, I admit it—they are special, and so I've carried on her tradition. I make them for my birthday and for Christmas tea—and for other special occasions, too.

INGREDIENTS:
2 cups sifted cake flour
2 teaspoons baking powder
½ teaspoon salt
2 teaspoons sugar
4 tablespoons butter
1 egg and 1 egg yolk well
    beaten
⅓ cup light cream
1 egg white, slightly beaten
sugar

Preheat oven to 450°. Sift flour once. Measure, add baking powder, salt, and sugar, and sift again. Cut in butter. Add egg and cream all at once and stir carefully until all flour is dampened. Then stir vigorously until mixture forms a soft dough. Turn out on slightly floured board and knead 30 seconds. Roll ½ inch thick and cut in triangles. Place on ungreased baking sheet. Brush tops lightly with egg white, and sprinkle with sugar. Bake 12 to 15 minutes.
Yield: 12 scones.

AUNT LIZZIE'S SCOTTISH SHORTBREAD

Christmas wouldn't be Christmas without shortbread. And, of course, a proper tea wouldn't be quite as proper without it, either.

INGREDIENTS
2 cups sifted all-purpose flour
¼ teaspoon salt
1 cup unsalted butter
½ cup granulated or confectioners' sugar

Preheat oven to 325°. Sift together the flour and salt. In a large mixing bowl, cream the butter and sugar together until they almost look white. Slowly add the flour mixture, mixing well. Press into an 8 x 8 x 2-inch pan until level and smooth. Using a fork, prick the entire surface. Bake for 30 minutes or until just starting to get golden brown. While still warm, cut into 2-inch pieces.
Yield: 16 bars.

CUCUMBER SANDWICHES

Okay, I know you're saying to yourself, "What could be easier to make than a cucumber sandwich? Why the need for a recipe?" Well, if you've never had one, you might want a few pointers.

And why are cucumber sandwiches so often associated with English teas? Well, they're small, dainty, and … cute!

INGREDIENTS
thin slices of white bread
1 English (seedless) cucumber
softened butter
pepper and salt (to taste)

Using thin white bread, spread the butter all the way to the edges of two slices. (This keeps the bread from getting soggy.) Thinly slice the cucumber and place on one piece of the bread. (You can do more than one layer if you prefer.) Lightly salt and pepper if so desired. Place the second piece of bread over the cucumbers. Slice off all the crust edges and cut the sandwich on the diagonal into quarters. (Feel free to make as many as you like for yourself, your family, or your guests.)
Yield: 1 sandwich.

EGG SALAD SANDWICHES

Another sandwich closely associated with an English tea is egg salad. This recipe is for one sandwich. Increase the number of eggs and other ingredients according to how many people you intend to feed.

INGREDIENTS

1 hard-boiled egg* (large), peeled and chopped
1-2 tablespoons mayonnaise (to taste)
2 tablespoons chopped celery
1 tablespoon chopped green onion (or one green
    queen olive)
salt and pepper (to taste)
1 leaf of lettuce
2 slices thinly sliced white bread

Mash up the chopped egg a bit. Mix together the chopped hard-boiled egg, mayonnaise, celery, and onion. Sprinkle with salt and pepper. Mix with a spoon. Using thin white bread, spread the butter all the way to the edges of two slices. (This keeps the bread from getting soggy.) Spread the egg mixture evenly across one of the buttered slices. Slice off all the crust edges and cut the sandwich on the diagonal into quarters.

Yield: 1 sandwich.

*OTHER SANDWICH IDEAS

The lovely thing about these dainty tea sandwiches is that you can mix the ingredients. Instead of cucumber, try thinly sliced smoked salmon. How about goat cheese, watercress, tuna salad, or anything you have hanging around the house. Be creative!

RAISIN SCONES

My aunt Lizzie made wonderful scones. She must have baked them at least two or three times a week—and we ate them for breakfast or tea. This is the recipe she used most often. It's easy and satisfying.

Ingredients
2 cups flour
¼ cup sugar
2 teaspoons baking powder
¾ teaspoon salt
3 tablespoons unsalted butter, cold
¾ cup milk
1 egg
½ cup raisins, sultanas, or currants
1 egg yolk
2 tablespoons cold water

Preheat oven to 350°.
Sift the dry ingredients together. Using a pastry blender or two knives, cut the butter into the dry ingredients until the mixture resembles crumbs. Beat the milk and whole egg together. Pour into the dry

ingredients and stir until well blended. Add the raisins, stirring until well mixed.

Sprinkle the flour over a flat surface. The dough will be rather wet and will absorb the flour. Briefly knead the dough (once or twice) and pat down until the dough is ¾-inch thick. Cut out the scones with a biscuit cutter and place on a greased cookie sheet.

Beat the egg yolk with the cold water. Brush glaze over the scones. Bake for 25-30 minutes or until golden brown.

Serve hot or cold with butter or clotted cream and jam.

Yield: 10-12 scones.

WALNUT SCONES

I got this recipe from a friend in college. Her mother always made them this way and, as she knew I liked to bake, she asked her mom to share the recipe with me.

INGREDIENTS
2 cups all-purpose flour
¼ cup granulated sugar
2 teaspoons baking powder
½ teaspoon salt
3 tablespoons butter, cold
¾ cup milk
1 egg
½ cup walnuts, coarsely chopped*
1 egg yolk
2 tablespoons cold water

Preheat oven to 350°. Sift the dry ingredients together. Using a pastry blender (or a fork), cut the butter into the dry ingredients until crumbly. Beat the milk and egg together. Pour into the dry ingredients, stirring until a dough forms. Add the chopped nuts, combining well. Using an ice cream scoop, form the scones and place them on an aluminum (or parchment paper) lined baking sheet. Beat the egg yolk with the cold water. Using a pastry brush, glaze each scone with this mixture. Bake for 25 to 30 minutes or until golden brown. Serve hot or cold. (Hot is better! *You can substitute pecans or any other nut you prefer. Pistachios make an interesting scone.)
Yield: 10-12 scones.

SCOTTISH DUNDEE CAKE

My aunt Lizzie used to make this cake at Christmas-time. It's always special.

INGREDIENTS
2 cups all-purpose flour
1 ½ teaspoons baking powder
¾ cup butter, room temperature
¾ cup granulated sugar
3 eggs, room temperature
½ cup orange marmalade
16 ounces mixed candied fruit
1 cup golden raisins
½ cup blanched almond slices
¼ cup brandy

Preheat oven to 300°. Grease a 2-inch deep by 8-inch cake pan and line it with waxed paper. Sift together flour and baking powder into a medium size bowl. Cream the butter and sugar in a large bowl until light and fluffy. Add eggs, one at a time, then marmalade. Gently fold in the flour mixture. Stir in the dried fruits and brandy, mixing well. Pour into the cake pan. Arrange the almonds in a circular pattern around the top. Brush with egg white. Bake for 2 ½ hours or until an inserted toothpick comes out clean. Cool in the pan for about an hour. Turn onto a wire rack. Yield: 12 servings.

TO TOP YOUR SCONES

What good are scones without butter, jam (my favorite is raspberry!), and clotted cream? Here's how my aunt Lizzie always made hers.

CLOTTED CREAM

INGREDIENT
2 cups heavy cream

Pour the cream into the top portion of a double boiler and cook until it is reduced to about half. It should be the consistency of butter, with a golden "crust" on the top.

Transfer the cream (including the crust) to a bowl. Cover and let stand for about two hours then refrigerate for at least 12 hours. Stir the crust into the cream before serving. (This also tastes good on crumpets and English muffins.)
Yield: 1 ¾ cups.

HONEY BUTTER

INGREDIENTS
1 cup unsalted butter,
    room temperature
¼ cup honey
¼ cup confectioners' sugar

In a medium bowl, mix the butter, honey, and confectioners' sugar together until fluffy. Store in the refrigerator until ready to serve. Use within 7 days.
Yield: 1 ½ cups.

LEMON CURD

INGREDIENTS
3 eggs
½ cup fresh lemon juice
½ cup confectioners' sugar
½ cup unsalted butter, melted
1 cup granulated sugar

In the top part of a double boiler, beat the eggs until frothy. Stir in the lemon juice, sugar, and melted butter. Place over simmering water. Stir constantly for about 20 minutes. The mixture should become slightly thickened. Remove from the heat and spoon into a pint-sized container. Cool to room temperature, cover and refrigerate for at least two hours before serving. Use within 14 days.
Yield: About 2 cups.

PEACH BUTTER

INGREDIENTS
1 cup unsalted butter, room temperature
¼ cup peach preserves
¼ cup confectioners' sugar

In a medium bowl, combine the butter, preserves, and

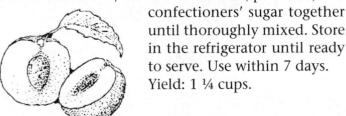

confectioners' sugar together until thoroughly mixed. Store in the refrigerator until ready to serve. Use within 7 days.
Yield: 1 ¼ cups.

VANILLA CREAM CHEESE

If you haven't got time to make clotted cream, a good second choice is vanilla cream cheese. In no time at all you'll be spreading this creamy mixture on your scones, crumpets, or English muffins, and enjoying it almost as much. The beauty of this easy recipe is you can change it by adding different flavors. I like using almond, orange, or lemon extracts, too.

INGREDIENTS
1 3-ounce package of cream cheese, softened
1 teaspoon of vanilla extract (or the extract of your choice)
2 tablespoons confectioners' sugar

Beat ingredients together just to combine. Transfer to a serving bowl.
Yield: ½ cup.

ABOUT THE AUTHOR

A native of Rochester, NY, Lorraine Bartlett honed her characterization and plotting skills writing short stories for magazines and was a finalist in the St. Martin's/Malice Domestic contest.

Ms. Bartlett also writes the New York Times Bestselling and Agatha-nominated Booktown Mystery series under the name of Lorna Barrett. *Bookplate Special*, the third book in the series, was nominated for an Agatha Award for best novel of 2009. As L.L. Bartlett, she writes the Jeff Resnick Mysteries.

Visit her website at:
http://www.lorrainebartlett.com/

You can also find her on Facebook, Goodreads, and Twitter (@LorraineBartlet).

INDEX

Printed in Great Britain
by Amazon